Sacralizing the Secular

acralizing
the Secular

THE RENAISSANCE ORIGINS OF

MODERNITY

Stephen A. McKnight

LOUISIANA STATE UNIVERSITY PRESS
Baton Rouge and London

99 98 97 96 95 94 93 92 91 90 89   5 4 3 2 1

Designer: Laura Roubique Gleason
Typeface: Palatino
Typesetter: The Composing Room of Michigan, Inc.
Printer: Thomson-Shore, Inc.
Binder: John H. Dekker & Sons, Inc.

Library of Congress Cataloging-in-Publication Data

McKnight, Stephen A., 1944–
    Sacralizing the secular : the Renaissance origins of modernity /
    Stephen A. McKnight.
        p.   cm.
    Bibliography: p.
    Includes index.
    ISBN 0-8071-1449-9 (alk. paper)
        1. Europe—Intellectual life.   2. Hermetism—Italy—Influence.
3. Philosophy, Renaissance.   4. Philosophy, Modern.   5. Humanism—
History.   6. Secularism—History.   7. Political science—History.
I. Title.
CB203.M35   1989
940.2—dc19   88-9048
                                                                  CIP

The paper in this book meets the guidelines for permanence and durability of the
Committee on Production Guidelines for Book Longevity of the Council on Library
Resources.∞

To the Memory of Two Extraordinary Scholars and Teachers

Eric Voegelin
and
Gregor Sebba

Contents

Preface and Acknowledgments

The research that led to the writing of this book began almost ten years ago and was stimulated by two developments in historical scholarship. The first was the increased attention given to ancient Gnosticism as a result of the final publication of the library at Nag Hammadi. This event was celebrated by international conferences that began the revaluation of Gnosticism's place in ancient religion, the history of Christianity, and its relation to modern thought and experience. My own interests were primarily with the last subject. Pioneering studies by Carl Jung in psychology, Hans Jonas in philosophy, and Eric Voegelin in political science had pointed to the important correlations between modern thought and experience and the myths and symbols of ancient Gnosticism. The new data generated an even wider interest in and application of this analysis. At the same time, specialists began to complain that the character of ancient Gnosticism was being distorted in order to draw parallels to modern psychology, philosophy, literary criticism, and political science.

While this renewed interest in Gnosticism was under way, another major scholarly development was also gaining momentum. This was the increasing recognition of the importance of what D. P. Walker called the *prisca theologia*, or Ancient Wisdom, tradition in Renaissance thought. This Ancient Wisdom includes a wide array of

esoteric religious and pseudo-scientific traditions that are now recognized as a valued part of the Renaissance recovery of ancient
learning. The analysis of these materials and the revaluation of their
impact on philosophy and theology were begun by historians of
science such as Lynn Thorndike and then carried forward by D. P.
Walker, Eugenio Garin, Frances Yates, and other Renaissance specialists. As I examined these works and the primary sources on
which they were based I became convinced that many features of
modern thought and experience that had been identified with ancient Gnosticism could more properly be traced to this Ancient
Wisdom tradition.

The Vanderbilt Conference on Gnosticism and Modernity, which
was organized by William C. Havard and Richard Bishirjian, provided me the first public opportunity to question prevailing views
on Gnosticism and modernity and to develop the significance of the
Ancient Wisdom materials. This conference was also important because Eric Voegelin, the keynote speaker, acknowledged that empirical and theoretical developments were changing the framework
for the analysis of modernity and that in light of new materials he
would place less emphasis on Gnosticism. Moreover, he specifically
identified the work that I was doing on the Renaissance Ancient
Wisdom as an important area of development.

This project was interrupted from 1981 through 1983 when I was
invited by the administration to serve as Director of the Office of
Academic Programs for the U.S. Information Agency. (This office
supervises most of the government's academic exchange programs,
including the Fulbright program.) When I returned to the University
of Florida and resumed work on the manuscript, I found that scholars' work on the Ancient Wisdom and its influence had expanded
considerably and that my own preliminary efforts had to be substantially revised and augmented. I am pleased to acknowledge the
generous support I received from my department chairman, David
R. Colburn; my dean, Charles F. Sidman; and the vice-president for
research, Donald F. Price. Also, I would like to express my appreciation to the Earhart Foundation for a fellowship for the summer of
1987. This support was crucial to my completing the manuscript on
time.

I also owe a debt to colleagues who were kind enough to read early drafts of the manuscript. I am particularly grateful to Robert Hatch and Frederick Conner for their advice and criticism.

For the preparation of the manuscript, I owe a debt of gratitude to the secretarial staff of my department; and for help with the Bibliography, I am indebted to Jay Malone. I owe a special debt of gratitude to my wife, Becky, who has typed, retyped, proofread, and reread draft after draft and page after page.

Finally, I want to express appreciation to Beverly Jarrett and LSU Press. LSU Press is, of course, Eric Voegelin's primary publisher, and Ms. Jarrett, who is Executive Editor and Associate Director, has served as his principal editor. While this is not a book on Voegelin, it does seek to advance the study of scholarly problems and issues that Voegelin's own work sought to address. It is an honor, therefore, to have the Press publish this study.

Sacralizing the Secular

Introduction

A NEW PERSPECTIVE ON THE MODERN AGE

This study draws upon recent Renaissance scholarship to develop a new perspective on three features associated with the meaning and use of the term *modernity* from the fourteenth century to the present. The first is an intense epochal consciousness of a decisive break with the preceding era. Corollary symbols describe this break as a "rebirth" after an age of sterility and death or an "enlightenment" after a "dark age." The second is the conviction that an epistemological breakthrough separates the vital era of enlightenment from the sterile age of darkness. While the specific ingredients in this epistemological leap change over the course of time, there is a general belief that humanity has acquired (or recovered) the knowledge needed to overcome its alienated condition and create a perfect society. The third element in this configuration is the accompanying conviction that man's new theoretical and instrumental knowledge provides the means of becoming completely autonomous and self-determining.

From this brief description, it should be clear that my purpose here is not to catalog the range of possible meanings of the terms *modernity* and *modern age* or to concoct a generic definition that would be sufficiently elastic to cover all possible uses the terms have acquired. Such efforts would not only be impossible to complete but would have virtually no scholarly application. My purpose instead is to demonstrate that this particular configuration is a fundamental component in Western thought and experience from the Renaissance to the present and to show how recent scholarly developments profoundly alter conventional interpretations of its origins and development.[1]

From as early as the seventeenth-century "Quarrel Between the Ancients and Moderns" through the eighteenth-century Enlightenment and the nineteenth-century "social science" movements, this epochal break has been associated with science and/or secularization.[2] *Science* in this context means the methods and models of Newtonian physics, which the "modernists" were convinced could serve as the basis for a new science of man, society, and history. *Secularization* is the term used to denote a wide range of intellectual, social, and political developments that undermined the ecclesiastical, theological, and political power of the Church and purportedly resulted in what Hans Blumenberg describes as man's "self-emancipation."[3]

New research challenges these conventional claims in two fundamental ways. First, historians of science have shown that the epistemological break that supposedly occurred through the Scientific Revolution is not as clear and as decisive as claimed. Revaluations of the interrelation of science and pseudo-science have demonstrated that magic and other esoteric traditions strongly affected Renaissance intellectual developments that contributed to the Scientific Revolution and that pseudo-science served as a chrysalis for the formulation of scientific concepts and procedures well into the eighteenth century.[4] Renaissance intellectual historians, following the

1. A brief concept history (*begriffsgeschichte*) is provided in Chapter One.

2. Comte's effort to develop a *physique sociale*, which uses the methods of the natural sciences to diagnose and reform society, is an example of this kind of "social science."

3. Hans Blumenberg, *The Legitimacy of the Modern Age*, trans. Robert M. Wallace (Cambridge, Mass., 1983).

4. *Pseudo-science* here refers to the various occult sciences, *i.e.*, magic and alchemy, and this usage is consistent with the history of science as found, for example, in *Isis*, a leading journal in the field. It should be noted that this term is being applied somewhat anachronistically, however. The formal distinction between empirical science and pseudo-science was not actually made until the seventeenth century. These occult sciences in the fifteenth and sixteenth centuries were regarded as pristine

path opened by historians of science, have substantially revised the place of the *prisca theologia, i.e.,* pseudo-science and esoteric religion, in the recovery of ancient learning and have shown their strong influence in the philosophical and theological ferment of the fifteenth and sixteenth centuries.[5]

Drawing on these recent developments, this study demonstrates that this *prisca theologia,* or Ancient Wisdom, tradition also contributes to the emerging epochal consciousness by introducing two major new concepts into Renaissance thought. The first is the concept of man as a "terrestrial God" who can shape his own destiny. The second is the epistemological shift that transforms magic into the "highest form of natural philosophy" because it provides the operative power to control nature and perfect society.[6] I will first show that these two concepts form the basis of the Neoplatonists' "new understanding of human nature" and then trace the transmission of this understanding into the utopian schemes of three patriarchs of modernity: Bacon, Comte, and Marx. My intent is to open a new line of investigation that parallels the recent work of historians of science. These scholars initiated an inquiry into the most fundamental assumptions about the nature of the Scientific Revolution and its relation to pseudo-science. As a result, they have been able to show that pseudo-science continued to be an influence on scientific developments into the eighteenth century. This study proposes to begin an examination of the influence of pseudo-science or the Ancient Wisdom tradition on the development of social science.

---

revelations provided by God. The term, though somewhat anachronistic, is useful for my purposes because I want to trace the influence of these traditions from the fifteenth century to the present and need a term that can be used throughout the analysis.

5. Although D. P. Walker introduced the terms *prisca theologia* and *prisci theologi* (ancient theologians) into current research, *prisca theologia* is a Renaissance term commonly used by Ficino and other Hermetists and Neoplatonists. It expresses their conviction that such wisdom was a pristine revelation by God to ancient non-Christian magi.

6. Both Ficino and Pico indicate that their purpose is to use the newly recovered ancient teachings to develop a new understanding of human nature. Ficino says as much in the introduction to the *Theologia Platonica* and also in a later chapter in which he describes man as a "terrestrial God" (Book XIX). Pico presents his new understanding in a remythologizing of the creation story in his *Oration on Human Dignity.*

Specifically, it intends to demonstrate that the epistemological conviction that knowledge supplies the operative means to change the human condition derives from Ficino's elevation of Hermetic magic, and it will also link Ficino's concept of the magus as a "terrestrial God" to views found in the works of Bacon, Comte, and Marx. The introduction of this new perspective also challenges the prevalent view of modernity as an essentially secular age. The claim of the secularists is that the modern age has liberated itself from irrational religious beliefs and naïve metaphysical speculation. This study demonstrates, however, that Hermetism and other esoteric religious traditions revived in the Renaissance shape the views of man and knowledge that are at the core of modern epochal consciousness.

Obviously, however, this study is not the first to challenge the equation of modernity with secularization by developing religious parallels. In fact, two long-standing scholarly traditions contend that modernity is based on a deformation of Christian views of society and history or maintain that modern thought shares fundamental experiences and symbols with ancient Gnostic religion. The first of these views is widely associated with Karl Löwith.[7] The second is identified with major figures in several fields, including Carl Jung in psychology, Hans Jonas in philosophy, Harold Bloom in literary criticism, and Eric Voegelin in political science.[8] It will become clear that the Ancient Wisdom materials and the theoretical

7. Löwith's most influential monograph is *Meaning in History: The Theological Implications of the Philosophy of History* (Chicago, 1949). His other important works include *Weltgeschichte und Heilgeschehen: Die theologischen Voraussetzungen der Geschichtsphilosophie* (2nd ed.; Stuttgart, 1953) and *From Hegel to Nietzsche: The Revolution in Nineteenth-Century Thought* (New York, 1964), David E. Green's translation of the 1941 original.

8. Jung's contribution includes several major publications and the Eranos Conferences, which brought prominent scholars together to discuss the implication of this material. Hans Jonas, the famous pupil of Heidegger's, has said that he found in ancient Gnosticism the key to understanding modern existentialism and nihilism. See Jonas, *Gnosis und spätantiker Geist* (2 vols.; Göttingen, 1934–54); and Jonas, *The Gnostic Religion: The Message of the Alien God and the Beginnings of Christianity* (2nd ed.; Boston, 1963). Several of Harold Bloom's works have explored Gnostic themes in literature, and he has even written a Gnostic fantasy: *The Flight to Lucifer* (New York, 1979). Eric Voegelin has written extensively on this subject. His major studies include *The New Science of Politics* (Chicago, 1952); *Science, Politics and Gnosticism* (Chicago, 1964); and *From Enlightenment to Revolution*, ed. John H. Hallowell (Durham, 1975).

perspective developed here have a direct bearing on these modes of interpretation and the scholarly debates surrounding them. These brief references to connections with established views lead to another basic point. A study proposing a new perspective on the origin and development of modern epochal consciousness has two principal tasks. The major one is to analyze primary materials to demonstrate the influence of the Ancient Wisdom tradition in the work of influential modern thinkers. Of course, a single study cannot provide a comprehensive analysis. It is possible, however, to select representative thinkers and works that are unquestionable contributors to modern thought and show the influence of the *prisca theologia* tradition. In developing this pattern of influence, I will examine the writings of Ficino, Pico, Agrippa, Bruno, Campanella, Bacon, Comte, and Marx.

The second obligation of a study of this kind is to relate its new perspective to established modes of interpretation. In this instance, there are two key connections to be made. The first is with the long-standing debate over secularization. For this purpose I will develop comparisons and contrasts with the widely discussed Löwith-Blumenberg debate over the nature of secularization and the "legitimacy of the modern age."[9] The second comparison will be with interpretations that draw parallels between modernity and ancient Gnosticism. Particular attention will be given to Eric Voegelin's analysis of epistemological parallels between the ancient doctrine of saving-knowledge (*gnosis*) and modern beliefs in the power of knowledge to transform and transcend the basic conditions of existence.[10]

9. The phrase "legitimacy of the modern age" is taken from the title of Hans Blumenberg's book. An English translation was prepared by R. M. Wallace and published by MIT Press in 1983. This text is based on the revised edition of *Die Legitimität der Neuzeit* (2nd ed.; Frankfurt am Main, 1976). The widespread interest in the secularization debate is evidenced by extended review of Blumenberg's work in philosophy, religion, and intellectual history journals such as *Religious Studies Review,* IV (1985), 165–70, and *Journal of Modern History,* LVI (1984), 698–701. Perhaps the most dramatic evidence of the interest in Blumenberg and the debate is found in a publisher's promotion of a book on Nicholas of Cusa that prominently claims to provide "the first serious American critique of Hans Blumenberg's *Die Legitimität der Neuzeit.*"

10. For a discussion of the main lines of this approach, see Voegelin, *Science, Politics and Gnosticism,* 1–12; and Gregor Sebba, "History, Modernity and Gnosticism," in Peter Opitz and Gregor Sebba (eds.), *The Philosophy of Order: Essays on History, Consciousness and Politics* (Stuttgart, 1981), 190–241.

Perhaps the best way to explain how these several topics are to be developed is to describe briefly each chapter. The first establishes the meaning and use of the primary concepts around which the new perspective is developed and identifies the principal connections between this approach and other modes of interpretation. The first term examined is *modernity*. A brief historical analysis demonstrates that the new epochal consciousness results in a fundamental change in traditional patterns of historical interpretation—one in which the categorical distinctions between sacred and secular history become obscured or obliterated. Next, the concept of secularization is examined. Through an investigation of the theoretical and methodological issues in the Löwith-Blumenberg controversy, it is possible to explain why the concept cannot accommodate the results of recent scholarship and why these developments make it necessary to introduce the opposite yet complementary concept of sacralization. This discussion will explain how the concept derives from the *prisca theologia* tradition and will demonstrate its influence on Renaissance thought.

The second chapter further develops the concepts of secularization and sacralization by demonstrating that both processes began in the Renaissance and led to a breakdown of the traditional Christian understanding of the interrelation of the sacred and the secular poles of human existence. So that the characteristic features of each process can be clearly understood, a detailed examination of texts reflecting each will be provided. The analysis of secularization focuses on the writings of Boccaccio, Machiavelli, and Galileo to demonstrate that secularization splits the two poles apart in an effort to establish the secular as an autonomous field. The examination of sacralization focuses on one of the Ancient Wisdom texts, the *Corpus Hermeticum*, to show that it is a key source for the Renaissance sacralizing pattern that obliterates distinctions between the secular and the sacred. As a result, man is depicted as a terrestrial god and society as an earthly paradise.

The third chapter traces the transmission of the sacralizing pattern from the Ancient Wisdom materials into the theological and philosophical writings of Ficino and Pico. The analysis of Ficino's thought centers on his "new understanding of human nature" presented in *The Platonic Theology (Theologia Platonica)* and his revolutionary claim that "magic is the highest form of natural philosophy" in *The Book of Life (De vita triplici)*. The study of Pico focuses on his *Oration on Human Dignity*, which Burckhardt and others have celebrated as the prototypical example of the emerging modern view of human dignity, autonomy, and creativity. What traditional scholarship has not properly recognized is that Pico regards man as "the great miracle" because he possesses magic and through it is able to attain self-divinization or sacralization.

The fourth chapter establishes the presence and influence of the sacralizing tradition within the intellectual ferment of the sixteenth and seventeenth centuries by examining the writings of three major figures: Agrippa, Bruno, and Campanella. The analysis of their writings shows that the emphasis of sacralization moves from Ficino's and Pico's efforts at self-divinization to utopian dreams of a priest-king who can overcome the religious disorder of the age and install a new political order.

The fifth chapter reexamines the work of three of the patriarchs of modernity: Bacon, Comte, and Marx. This analysis shows that in addition to the familiar secular elements in their writings, there is a sacralizing pattern as well. The purpose of this examination is to provide a further illustration of how a rereading of major modern texts is necessary in light of new insights into the influence of the *prisca theologia* tradition on the main lines of modern thought. This revaluation is aimed specifically at the origins of the modern epistemological linking of knowledge with the operative power to control nature and to perfect society. Modern reformers such as Bacon, Comte, and Marx claim that their programs for social improvement derive from natural science. New evidence, however, demonstrates close parallels to the sacralizing aims of the pseudo-sciences of magic and alchemy.

The Conclusion has two purposes. It draws together the results of this study's efforts to open new perspectives on modernity and to clarify the roles of secularization and sacralization. It also identifies three emerging fields of research crucial to furthering the analysis of modernity.

One further note about format needs to be added. Because this study integrates research from several disciplines, readers may not be familiar with some materials and scholarly traditions covered. Therefore, the footnotes will augment the analysis in the narrative of each chapter by identifying the sources most directly influencing the position being developed or by citing significant modes of interpretation that contrast sharply with the theoretical approach and historical perspective introduced. In addition, the Bibliography is arranged topically to list pertinent scholarship on the major sources and themes covered.

Chapter One

SECULARIZING AND SACRALIZING PATTERNS IN MODERNITY

The most distinctive feature of modernity is the underlying conviction that an epochal break separates it from the preceding "dark age." Integral to this epochal consciousness is a new confidence in man's capacity for self-determination, and this in turn derives from the conviction that an epistemological breakthrough provides man with the capacity to change the conditions of his existence. As we follow the stages in the development of the concept of modernity, we also find a breakdown of distinctions between sacred and secular history that leads to a reformulation of the traditional pattern of Western historiography. And, as we shall see, this poses fundamental questions about the influence of secularization and sacralization.

MODERNITY

The first major figure to express the new epochal consciousness was Petrarch (1304–1374), who juxtaposed the dawn of the new age to the dark age that was at last coming to an end. Petrarch also provides the first formulation of a three-phase history moving from a classical period through a Christian dark age to the modern age of humanity's rebirth and renewal.[1] His revolutionary interpretation

1. Petrarch is, of course, not the only developer of a three-stage construction of history that has formal connections with eighteenth- and nineteenth-century pro-

of the stages of Western history was evidently precipitated by his trip to Rome for his coronation as poet laureate in April, 1341. His correspondence shows that he was awed by the sight of the civilizational remnants from the imperial period, which preceded the establishment of Christianity as the religion of the empire.[2] For Petrarch, the stone and marble monuments stood as imperishable testimony to both the nobility of man and the majesty of his cultural and political achievements. In an effort to reawaken the consciousness of the dignity and the creativity of man reflected in the grandeur of the Roman monuments, Petrarch proposed to prepare a history that would highlight this period and distinguish it from the period of darkness (*età tenebrae*) that followed "the celebration of the name of Christ in Rome."[3] This formulation is extraordinary for his era; it is the first time that the term *dark age* is used to refer to the period of the Christian empire. In fact, this characterization inverts the standard periodization of history that contrasts the age of Christianity to the preceding age of pagan darkness. In his famous poem, the *Africa*, Petrarch develops this imagery further and says: "My fate is to live amid varied and confusing storms. But for you perhaps, if as I hope and wish you will live long after me, there will follow a better age. This sleep of forgetfulness will not last forever. When the darkness has been dispersed, our descendants can shine again in

---

gressivist constructions. Scholars have also shown important parallels with Joachim of Fiore's (*ca.* 1132–1202) famous three stages of spiritual evolution and perfection. Petrarch is, however, the first to develop the historical pattern with the specific features we are examining, *i.e.*, a qualitative break between the Christian "dark age" and the modern age in which the source of meaning and purpose in history is transferred to man. Joachim, on the other hand, describes three progressive stages of spiritual enlightenment. For a discussion of Joachim's concept of history and its influence, see Marjorie Reeves, *Joachim of Fiore and the Prophetic Future* (London, 1976); Voegelin, *The New Science of Politics*, 110–121; and Löwith, *Meaning in History*, 145–59.

2. For a discussion of the correspondence in which this statement occurs, see Theodor Mommsen, "Petrarch's Concept of the 'Dark Age,'" in his *Medieval and Renaissance Studies*, ed. Eugene Rice, Jr. (Ithaca, 1959), 106–29. At this point, Petrarch identifies only two historical periods because he has not yet differentiated the contemporary period (*età moderna*) from the continuation of this dark age.

3. For the quotation and an analysis, see Mommsen, "Petrarch's Concept of the 'Dark Age,'" 127.

the form of pure radiance."[4] In expressing this hope, Petrarch is now distinguishing three periods in Western history—the classical age, the dark age, and the emerging modern epoch.

In developing this pattern, Petrarch introduces two major innovations in Western historiography. First, he has changed the conventional model that divided Western history into two epochs, the ancient and the modern. Second, he has transformed the site and source of the basic epochal distinction. In conventional history, the coming of Christ and the establishment of Christianity as an ecumenic religion divided the ancient and modern periods. In this formulation the period before the birth of Christ is referred to as a dark age. In Petrarch's conception, the age of darkness begins with the establishment of the Christian religion in Rome, and the modern period begins with a reawakening consciousness of the grandeur of Western civilization and the majesty of the human spirit. Petrarch's formulation, then, is the first instance of the three-stage pattern of history that separates two periods of light by a period of darkness. Petrarch's reconceptualization would not be of great significance if it remained restricted to his own work or even to his own time. But this characterization supplies the root symbols of the Enlightenment and introduces the historical pattern that has dominated Western historiography down to recent times.

While Petrarch viewed his own time as the tenuous beginning of the transition from darkness to light, later Renaissance humanists spoke confidently of their own age as one of "rebirth" and even proclaimed the accomplishments of its greatest figures to be superior to achievements during the classical age.[5] The historian who first uses the term *la rinascita* to distinguish his age from the preceding age of sterility and death was the sixteenth-century historian

4. Petrarch, *Africa*, IX, 451–57. See Mommsen, "Petrarch's Concept of the 'Dark Age,'" 127f.

5. For a discussion of Renaissance historiography, see W. K. Ferguson, "The Interpretation of the Renaissance," in P. O. Kristeller and P. P. Wiener (eds.), *Renaissance Essays: From the Journal of the History of Ideas* (New York, 1968); and Erwin Panofsky, *Renaissance and Renascences in Western Art* (Stockholm, 1960), esp. Chap. 1, "Renaissance—Self-Definition or Self-Deception."

Vasari.[6] His *Lives of the Most Excellent Italian Painters, Sculptors, and Architects* is more than the first "modern art history," as it is often described. For Vasari and many of his contemporaries, art represented the highest form of human creativity.[7] Therefore, his record of the achievements of Leonardo and Michelangelo, whom he regards as the greatest artists who ever lived, is a demonstration of a burgeoning human creativity that leads to a thoroughgoing cultural renewal and revitalization.

Vasari's designation of this new era as a period of renaissance marks another significant appropriation of religious imagery and another blurring of categorical distinctions between the sacred and the secular. Petrarch had borrowed and reversed the distinction between the age of darkness and the age of light. Vasari draws upon the conversion imagery of resurrection and rebirth but applies it to a cultural rather than a spiritual revitalization. Prior to Vasari's formulation, there had been references to other cultural renewals, for example, the Carolingian era; but contemporary interpreters regarded these as a revitalization (*renovatio*) and not as a revolutionary epochal break. The basic framework in which society was understood was not questioned, and the conventional historical pattern was not broken by these events. Vasari's formulation, by contrast, presents the new age as a radical departure from the Christian (Gothic) period. Moreover, his application of the language of salvation to secular developments marks an extraordinary inversion of sacred and secular history paralleling Petrarch's inversion of the periods of darkness and light.

Another important feature of Vasari's historiographical innovations is his alteration of the conventional analogy of the history of a culture to the biological cycles of birth and death. Greek and Roman historians had traced the rise and fall of known cultures, referring to movement from infancy through childhood to adulthood and finally old age and death. Vasari traces the infancy of the Renais-

6. See Panofsky's discussion in *Renaissance and Renascences*, 31ff.
7. For a discussion of the Neoplatonic view of the artist as magus, see E. H. Gombrich, *Symbolic Images: Studies in the Art of the Renaissance* (2nd ed.; Oxford, 1978); and Erwin Panofsky, *Studies in Iconology: Humanistic Themes in the Art of the Renaissance* (1939; rpr. New York, 1962).

sance from the work of Giotto through the transition in Masaccio (*adolescentia*) to its maturity in the work of Leonardo and Michelangelo. There is no discussion of the fourth and final stage (*senectus*), however, because Vasari finds no inherent reason that this extraordinary artistic achievement would go into decline.[8] The only precedent for Vasari's treatment is found in Christian salvation history (*heilsgeschichte*), which purposely uses the truncated pattern to mark the essential contrast between sacred and profane history. Tertullian, for example, describes three phases of religious and spiritual evolution culminating in "the Paracletan period," a period of spiritual maturity that will endure forever. Saint Augustine contrasts the City of God to the City of Man by stopping the cyclical pattern with the third stage of maturity because the City of God can never reach a period of senility and death.[9] With Vasari, then, we find another instance in which the modern epochal consciousness is expressed in a historical pattern that had been reserved for religious history. For Vasari, Petrarch, and other Renaissance revisionists seeking to mark the uniqueness of the events unfolding in their own time, conventional secular historical patterns were inadequate. Their experience could only be expressed in the language of conversion and spiritual awakening.

In the seventeenth century the consciousness of an epochal break with the past intensified and with ironic results. The central event is the scientific revolution, which divides the intellectual camp into "the ancients and the moderns."[10] In the early stages, the modernists would concede to the ancients that classical civilization had impressive achievements in politics, culture, and philosophy and

8. Vasari does express some anxiety that another period of barbarity might disrupt this age. But such a threat is external. In terms of the biological analogy, it is like saying an adult would never die unless murdered.

9. For a brief discussion, see Erwin Panofsky, *Meaning in the Visual Arts: Papers in and on Art History* (Garden City, N.Y., 1955), 219ff.

10. For an overview of the main lines of the argument, see J. B. Bury, *The Idea of Progress: An Inquiry into Its Origin and Growth* (New York, 1932), 78–97; and Richard F. Jones, *Ancients and Moderns: A Study of the Rise of the Scientific Movement in Seventeenth-Century England* (2nd ed.; St. Louis, 1961). For a useful discussion of the topic's relation to the development of a modern epochal consciousness, see Tilo Schabert, *Gewalt und Humanität: Ueber philosophische und politische Manifestationen von Modernität* (Freiburg, 1978), 51–68.

would grant that the principles established and the models provided continued to set the standards in those fields. Soon, however,
modernists became convinced that the basic principles of natural
science were applicable to every area of human endeavor and could
produce new insights into human nature and society. As a result,
ignorant and distorted conceptions could be overcome and true
knowledge attained. Of course, when the split becomes this pronounced, "modernists," like Petrarch and Vasari, who are so instrumental in the founding of the age and in articulating its epochal
consciousness, are exiled to the camp of the ancients. Sometimes
they are given an elevated status in the "dark ages" because they
have advanced somewhat beyond the superstition and negativism
of the Christian religion. Ultimately, however, they are relegated to
the ancient period because their efforts do not rest upon a scientific
base.

By the eighteenth century the accumulated pressures to integrate
the recent political, cultural, and intellectual advances into a coherent, intelligible pattern of historical development became a major preoccupation. Voltaire's proposal to develop a "philosophy of
history" to replace the outmoded theology of history is emblematic
of the direction taken.[11] Voltaire and his contemporaries shifted the
focus of history from the saving acts of the Judaeo-Christian God to
the unfolding progress of human reason and morality. In the nineteenth century, Auguste Comte refined the eighteenth-century
model and presented the famous three-stage pattern of historical
evolution that supplied the basic historiographical model for most
of the nineteenth and twentieth centuries. This Comtean paradigm,
like the Vasarian prototype, traces three stages in the maturation of
human consciousness from its infancy in religion through its metaphysical adolescence to its scientific maturity.

From this brief treatment of the root experiences and ideas associated with the concept of modernity, we can understand why it has
been linked so closely to secularization. From the outset, the modern epoch has been juxtaposed to the dark ages of Christianity. The
"rebirth" is expressed as a renewal of man's confidence in himself

11. Voltaire makes this distinction in his *Essay on the Manners and Mind of Nations*
[Essai sur les moeurs et l'esprit des nations] of 1756.

and in his capacities for finding meaning, purpose, and enjoyment in the here and now (*saeculum*). At the same time, this analysis also indicates that there is more to modern consciousness than this. The advances are experienced as being so significant and so profound that they defy placement within conventional patterns of secular history. The only suitable language to describe the epochal break-through is that of conversion and salvation. Moreover, the only usable historical pattern is the one borrowed from religious salvation history. The result of the adoption and transformation of these symbols and patterns is that the site of man's fulfillment is trans-ferred from the transcendent Kingdom of God to existence in this world; and the primary actor responsible for this achievement is man himself. This reconceptualization does not reflect a breaking away of the secular from the sacred. Instead, it shows an immanent-ization that blurs the fundamental distinctions between the sacred and the secular. Where Christian theologians and historians had distinguished the City of God from the City of Man, the pro-gressivist historian irradicated that distinction and employed the formerly sacred categories to describe the true character of life in the world.

The discussion of sacralization that follows will show how this immanentized view derives from the myths and symbols of the Ancient Wisdom tradition. First, however, it is important to explain more fully the theoretical and methodological problems surround-ing the effort to equate modernity with secularization.

SECULARIZATION

Recent concept histories (*begriffsgeschichten*) have shown that there has been a long-standing debate over the nature of secularization and that this conflict has directly affected the understanding of the character of modernity.[12] The term *secularization* derives its current usage from the seventeenth- and eighteenth-century clashes be-tween the emerging nation-states and the Church over the right to ownership of property within the boundaries of the state. States claimed the right to "secularize" Church holdings even if that meant

12. The principal studies are listed in the Bibliography under "Secularization and Modernity."

forced expropriation. The Church, on the other hand, maintained that this secularization was an unlawful violation of its authority and was finally an act of blasphemy against God.[13] From this specific context the term began to be used in an expanded, metaphorical way to designate the wholesale shift in the understanding of God and man, world and society, that distinguished the modern epoch from the preceding one. It was also from this point that the debate over the "legitimacy" of the modern age began. For the "modernists," secularization referred to the emancipation of man, society, and the world from ecclesiastical and theological domination. The critics of modernity saw in the secularizing movement—particularly in the doctrines of progress and social perfectibility—an effort to transform man into God and society into the Kingdom of God. This effort, the critics argued, constituted a blasphemous misconstruction of reality and a deformation of the understanding of human nature and society.

This dispute over the nature of secularization continues in the current debate over the nature of the modern age and is at the heart of the well-known Löwith-Blumenberg controversy.[14] Blumenberg maintains that legitimizing the basic character of modernity depends on a repudiation of the position represented by Löwith's work, which has "had such a protracted dogmatizing effect" that the attribute of illegitimacy has become a characteristic mark of both secularization and modernity.[15] In order to understand Blumenberg's criticisms and his proposed innovations, we need, therefore, to sketch Löwith's thesis.

Löwith's best-known work, *Meaning in History*, argues that the progressivist constructions of history that dominate the eighteenth

13. The term *secularization* appears in the formal negotiations preceding the Peace of Westphalia (1648). The attribute of "illegitimacy" is established in the "Final Resolution of the Reichstag's Special Commission (Reichsdeputationshauptschluss) of 1803." *Cf.* M. Stallman, *Was ist Säkularisierung?* (Tübingeny, 1960), 5–12; and Hermann Lübbe, *Sakularisierung: Geschichte eines ideenpolitischen Begriffs* (Freiburg, 1965), 28–29.

14. Blumenberg outlined his argument at the Seventh German Philosophy Congress in 1962 and published *Die Legitimität der Neuzeit* in 1966. This text was revised in 1976 to incorporate responses to questions and criticisms raised by reviewers and critics. The English translation used here is based on the revised edition.

15. Blumenberg, *The Legitimacy*, 27.

and nineteenth centuries closely parallel the patterns of Christian salvation history—with one basic difference. Man, rather than God, is the primary actor in the drama of salvation. In Christian *heilsgeschichte* the goal (*telos*) of history is to deliver man from ignorance and alienation in order that he may be admitted to the Kingdom of God. The primary events are God's revelation of the requirements for salvation and his merciful actions on behalf of sinful man. According to Löwith, the new "philosophies of history" follow the same pattern of progressive movement from ignorance and error to a reorientation in which mankind overcomes its alienation and is able to attain an enduring happiness. The principal difference between the sacred and the secular salvation stories is that the secular substitutes man as the primary actor. The events in this new salvation drama center on the evolution of human reason and morality. For Löwith, these progressivist constructions are "illegitimate" because they envision an innerworldly perfection that is impossible to attain. In order for man to obtain the knowledge necessary to reform human nature and perfect society, he would have to become God. Since man cannot escape his finitude or overcome his ultimate ontological ignorance, Löwith finds these efforts to secularize *heilsgeschichte* inappropriate and illegitimate. For him, the expropriation and secularization of theological concepts and patterns result in a deformed construction of reality and in a profound misunderstanding of the human condition.[16]

While this sketch cannot do justice to Löwith's position, it serves adequately as a background for understanding Blumenberg's criticisms. Blumenberg argues that there are three fundamental theoretical and methodological flaws. First, Löwith's "thesis that modern historical consciousness is derived from the Christian idea of salvation history" is a monochromatic reduction of many influences shaping modernity.[17] Second, Löwith fails to explain how the transcendent Christian pattern of *heilsgeschichte* becomes immanentized. Nor does he point out the stages of this transformation within

---

16. Löwith, *Meaning in History*. This analysis is expanded in the German work *Weltgeschichte und Heilgeschehen*. Blumenberg's analysis, however, refers to the more compact English work.

17. Blumenberg, *The Legitimacy*, 27ff.

the main lines of intellectual history from the medieval period to the modern age. "Regarding the dependence of the idea of progress on Christian eschatology, there are differences that would have had to block any transposition of the one into the other. It is a formal, but for that very reason a manifest, difference that an eschatology speaks of an event breaking into history, an event that transcends and is heterogeneous to it, while the idea of progress extrapolates from a structure present in every moment to a future that is immanent in history."[18] Third, Löwith has overestimated the significance of the eighteenth- and nineteenth-century constructions of history for understanding the character of modernity. These progressivist constructions, according to Blumenberg, are the result of outmoded conceptions carried over from the previous religious age and are not characteristic of the new modern consciousness.[19] Instead, they only confuse and discredit the legitimate basis for confidence in social and technological progress.

Blumenberg's criticisms are important for us to consider because they not only bring to light the basic issues in current scholarship but also allow us to establish the relation of this study to contemporary efforts to analyze the origin and character of modernity. While it can be argued that Blumenberg's reading of Löwith is unsympathetic and distorted, the general point in his first criticism is valid. The primary patterns of historical interpretation on both sides of the secularization debate hinge on the identification of the beginning and end of the dark age and the age of light. For the advocates of modernity, the dark age is identified with medieval Christendom. For the critics of modernity, the age of enlightenment is the age of darkness; and the Christian era, the age of light. Blumenberg is right to challenge the validity of such a pattern, but his appeal to historical data demonstrating a wide range of shaping influences also poses fundamental problems for his own position. In attempting to legitimize the modern age, Blumenberg disregards the influence of Western religious traditions. But this position stands in contradiction to the widening and deepening understanding of the roles played by a

18. *Ibid.*, 30.
19. See Blumenberg's discussion of the problems posed by attempting to "reoccupy outmoded positions," in *The Legitimacy,* 127ff.

complex array of religious traditions, including the Ancient Wisdom traditions. To disregard them in order to establish a monochromatic secularizing pattern is as "illegitimate" as is the effort to derive modernity solely from a misconstruction of Christian *heilsgeschichte*. Blumenberg's second criticism is the crucial one. He rightly underscores the profound differences between the modern dream of innerworldly fulfillment and the Christian concept of *heilsgeschichte* that places man's fulfillment beyond time and history. Blumenberg also correctly contends that such a profound transformation—if it did occur—should be demonstrable within the main lines of Western thought and experience. Blumenberg's valid criticisms do not lead, however, to valid theoretical conclusions. He maintains that the failure to be able to demonstrate these transformations invalidates the basic argument that modern dreams of innerworldly fulfillment are closely connected to religious dreams of human perfection. There is now evidence of an inherently immanentist view of man and society that derives from the Ancient Wisdom tradition. Moreover, this pattern contains fundamental elements of modern consciousness and can be documented as a key shaping force from the fifteenth century to the present.

Third, Blumenberg contends that the progressivist constructions of history that Löwith devotes his analysis to are not significant elements of modern epochal consciousness. Instead, he characterizes them as flawed efforts to answer "antiquated questions and reoccupy outmoded positions."[20] According to the history of the term *modernity* given herein, however, Blumenberg's position is indefensible. These constructions articulate the characteristic features of modern epochal consciousness from the Renaissance through to our own time. They are not incidental to the character of modernity; they are its very heart and core.

Blumenberg moves from these criticisms to develop a positive basis for understanding secularization and for associating it with the "progress" that separates modernity from the Middle Ages.[21] While

20. *Ibid.*
21. I am restricting my analysis to the theoretical underpinnings of Blumenberg's position; it is beyond the scope of this discussion to examine the merits of his historical analysis.

he provides valuable insights into the economic, social, and intellectual foundations of secularization, Blumenberg does not achieve his
primary goal of setting a new foundation for the understanding of
modernity. At the theoretical and methodological level, the study
remains tied to the polemical clash over the nature of secularization
that dates back to the eighteenth century. At the empirical level, the
study fails to take into account historical materials that have a direct
bearing on understanding the character of the age. If a genuine
theoretical and empirical advance is to be made, the monochromatic
linking of modernity with secularization must be set aside, and
adequate categories found for the integration of relevant historical
materials.[22] One important step in this direction is to introduce the
opposite yet complementary concept of sacralization.

SACRALIZATION

The principal myths and symbols of sacralization enter into modern
thought and experience through the Renaissance revival of the
prisca theologia tradition. While we know that most of the materials in
the Ancient Wisdom tradition appear late in the Hellenistic period,
the philosophers and theologians of the Renaissance understood
them to be the earliest and the most complete revelations to non-
Christian wise men (*prisci theologi*), for example, Pythagoras and
Zoroaster.[23] In the fifteenth century the teachings of Hermes Trismegistus came to be the most highly revered of all the ancient revelations. Through a curious set of circumstances, he even gained a
reputation as the spiritual mentor of both Moses and Plato; and his

22. Questions are also being raised about the theoretical validity of the concept of
secularization in sociology and the sociology of religion. David Martin has proposed
that the empirical data contradict the general theory of secularization and, therefore,
"*secularization* should be erased from the sociological dictionary" (*The Religious and the
Secular: Studies in Secularization* [New York, 1969], 22). See also David Martin, *A
General Theory of Secularization* (New York, 1978). While his theoretical and empirical
objections have a different source from those discussed here, the basic criticism is
similar. For a helpful overview of the history and current use of "the myth of secularization," see Harry J. Ausmus, *The Polite Escape: On the Myth of Secularization* (Athens, Ohio, 1982).

23. For a fuller discussion of the origins and character of the Ancient Wisdom, see
D. P. Walker, *Spiritual and Demonic Magic from Ficino to Campanella* (1958; rpr. London,
1969), 1–25; and Walker, *The Ancient Theology: Studies in Christian Platonism from the
Fifteenth to the Eighteenth Century* (Ithaca, 1972), 1–42.

teachings were, therefore, prized as the connecting link between Judaeo-Christian theology and classical philosophy.[24]

Initially, the Renaissance theologians' and philosophers' objective in studying the Ancient Wisdom was to establish the unifying core of these revelations and demonstrate their compatability with Christian truth. A growing conviction developed, however, that the *prisca theologia* contained a purer and deeper truth about man, God, society, and the world than was found in Christian theology or classical philosophy. By the sixteenth century, the Ancient Wisdom was a fundamental element in the mounting criticism of traditional theology and metaphysics and in the call for a thoroughgoing religious reorientation and political reformation. As we shall see, myths and symbols from the Ancient Wisdom tradition are found in the utopian dreams of social perfection that develop in the sixteenth and seventeenth centuries and the programs of social reformation in the eighteenth and nineteenth centuries.

If the sacralizing tradition is this fundamental, then why have scholars only recently begun to recognize its distinctive character and influence? Unfortunately, there is no adequate answer to this intriguing and perplexing question.[25] There is, however, a related and equally important question that can be at least partially answered: how and why did this field come to interest major Renaissance scholars such as Eugenio Garin, D. P. Walker, and Frances Yates?[26] Interestingly enough, it appears that the initial impetus did

24. See Frances Yates, *Giordano Bruno and the Hermetic Tradition* (London, 1964), 5f.; and Wayne Shumaker, *The Occult Sciences in the Renaissance: A Study in Intellectual Patterns* (Berkeley, 1972), for a brief introduction. The standard commentary on the Hermetic writings is A. J. Festugière, *La Révélation d'Hermès Trismégiste* (4 vols.; Paris, 1949–54).

25. Part of the explanation is in the concept of modernity itself. As we have seen, the epochal experience has produced patterns of historical interpretation that reinforce this basic concept. Much of Renaissance scholarship has sought to confirm the Renaissance origins of the modern emphasis on human dignity, creativity, and self-determination. Several scholars have pointed to the problems with this selective reading of Renaissance texts. One of the first is Eugenio Garin, *Medioevo e Rinascimento: Studi e ricerche* (Bari, 1954), esp. 90–99, 151–69, 170–91. See also William G. Craven, *Giovanni Pico della Mirandola: Symbol of His Age: Modern Interpretations of a Renaissance Philosopher* (Geneva, 1981).

26. For the studies that have led the way in opening the new perspective on Renaissance thought and experience, see the section "General Scholarship" in the Bibliography under "Renaissance."

not come from within Renaissance scholarship but from studies in the related fields of the history of science and the history of religion.

In recent years, historians of science have reexamined the long-standing claim that experimental science makes a clear, decisive break from the orientation, perspectives, and procedures of theology and natural philosophy. A pioneering study in this regard is Lynn Thorndike's eight-volume *History of Magic and Experimental Science* (1923–1958), but it carried the investigation in unexpected directions. In examining the factors that contributed to the breakdown of scholasticism and medieval Aristotelianism, Thorndike found that Hermetism, alchemy, and other systems of esoteric knowledge revived by Renaissance Neoplatonists played a fundamental role. Three of his eight volumes provide detailed accounts of the elevation of magic to the highest form of natural philosophy by Ficino and other Neoplatonists in the fifteenth, sixteenth, and seventeenth centuries. Thorndike's work set the context for Garin's, Walker's, and Yates's reassessments of the main lines of development in Renaissance thought and experience. Their studies have shown that these occult traditions had a broad-based impact on the Renaissance views of man, God, and the world.

More recent studies in the history of science have shown that the pseudo-sciences continued to be influential well into the seventeenth century.[27] As a result, these studies have further undercut the original premise that the beginnings of modern empirical, scientific, and inductive methods can be clearly differentiated from medieval and Renaissance theology, pseudo-science, and occult philosophy. These revaluations by historians of science point the way toward the general and much-needed revaluation of the relative influence of science and pseudo-science on the intellectual foundations of the modern epoch as a whole.

Developments in the history of religion have also helped to open the inquiry into pseudo-scientific and esoteric dimensions of modern thought and experience. One of the most significant areas of study has been in similarities between modernity and ancient Gnosticism. Carl Jung, for example, discovered fascinating parallels

27. See, for example, Betty J. Dobbs, *The Foundations of Newton's Alchemy: or, "The Hunting of the Greene Lyon"* (Cambridge, Mass., 1975).

between the Gnostic symbols and the dreams his modern patients had.[28] Similarly, Heidegger's famous student Hans Jonas found in these materials the clue to understanding the experiential basis of modern existentialism.[29] Eric Voegelin investigated the equivalences of experience and symbolization between the Gnostic doctrine of saving-knowledge (*gnosis*) and the modern belief that knowledge provides the power to transform the human condition.[30] More recently, literary critics as different as Cleanth Brooks and Harold Bloom have found ancient Gnosticism a useful tool in understanding modern literature.[31]

This exploration of parallels between Gnosticism and modernity also stimulated interest in the historical lines of transmission of the Gnostic myths and symbols, and this led to significant reassessment of the Renaissance revival of ancient learning. One of the most important of these studies is Festugière's translation and commentary on the primary Hermetic writings, the *Corpus Hermeticum*, which has influenced the work of Garin, Yates, Walker, and other Renaissance scholars.

Scholarship has now reached the point, however, where a careful discrimination needs to be made between Gnosticism and other esoteric components of the *prisca theologia* tradition. When Festugière, Yates, and others refer to the *Corpus Hermeticum* as a Gnostic text, they are using the term in its most general sense of salvation through knowledge. Used in this way, the term can apply not only to the ancient Gnostic religion, which has interested many analysts of modernity, but also to the wide array of esoteric traditions found in the Ancient Wisdom. Unfortunately, this general use obscures important distinctions between the specific features of ancient Gnostic religion and other traditions that are also based on a belief in salvation through knowledge. The basic difference is in world view.

28. Jung was instrumental in making the Nag Hammadi materials available and through his Eranos Conferences stimulated discussion and analysis.
29. See Jonas, *The Gnostic Religion*.
30. See, for example, Voegelin, *Science, Politics and Gnosticism;* and Sebba, "History, Modernity and Gnosticism," in Opitz and Sebba (eds.), *The Philosophy of Order*, 190–241.
31. Cleanth Brooks, "Walker Percy and Modern Gnosticism," *Southern Review*, XIII (1977), 677–87. Several of Bloom's critical works employ Gnosticism or the Cabala.

Ancient Gnosticism is a radically dualistic religion that describes the world as a prison and believes that salvation depends on escape from it. Other traditions, however, share the concept of salvation through knowledge but not this radical dualism. Portions of the Ancient Wisdom are immanentist, depicting man as a terrestrial god capable of creating paradise on earth.

These immanentist traditions are the source of the sacralizing pattern's emphasis on man as a magus who can control nature and perfect society. Consequently, the role of Gnosticism must be revaluated and revised.[32] This revaluation is particularly relevant to Voegelin's investigation of parallels between ancient Gnosticism and the modern linking of knowledge with the power to transform the human condition. Voegelin's position has been criticized because the radical dualism of ancient Gnostic religion is fundamentally different from the modern emphasis on innerworldly fulfillment. In fact, ancient Gnosticism regards the belief in innerworldly perfection to be the profoundest form of ignorance (*agnoia*). How, then, Voegelin's critics ask, can it be connected to modernity? When the historical base is expanded to include the immanentist Ancient Wisdom materials, the theoretical and methodological objections to Voegelin's and Löwith's positions can be overcome because these materials contain conceptions of man, of knowledge, and of society that conform to the immanentism of the modern age. Moreover, the expansion of the historical base to incorporate the cumulative findings of scholars in the history of science, Renaissance intellectual history, and the history of religion provides ample evidence to demonstrate that the sacralizing tradition plays as substantial a role in the shaping of modern thought and experience as does secularization.

32. Blumenberg makes positive references to the contribution of Gnosticism to modernity. No discussion is provided here because Blumenberg's position is flawed in the ways described earlier.

Chapter Two

SECULARIZATION AND SACRALIZATION
IN THE RENAISSANCE

Sacralization, like secularization, enters the mainstream of modern thought and experience during the Renaissance. Each produces a fundamental alteration of medieval Christian views of human nature, society, and God. Secularization results in independence and autonomy from God and the sacred. Sacralization transforms the secular realm to the point where it is indistinguishable from the sacred. Man becomes God, and society becomes an earthly paradise.

In order to see clearly the effect of each process, it is necessary to develop briefly the medieval Christian view of human nature. While there is great variety within Christian thought, there is general agreement that human existence has both a sacred and a secular dimension. The fundamental decisions in life involve choosing between the pulls and counterpulls of these two poles. The site of this struggle is the soul, and the nature of the conflict is articulated as the battle of reason and revelation against instinct and appetite or as the subjugation of the physical by the spiritual. The conflicts in this Christian psychomachia can be presented as follows:

Human Existence

Sacred	(Soul)	*Secular*
divine		animalic
(reason/revelation)		(appetite/instinct)

(continued)

spiritual	material
infinite	finite
transcendent	mundane
eternal	temporal

SECULARIZING PATTERNS IN THE RENAISSANCE

The secularized view of human nature minimizes or altogether ignores the sacred in favor of the physical and material. While Christian theology would regard this as a truncated, distorted view of man, the Renaissance secularizing tradition regards it as a breakthrough in human self-understanding. Three quite different advocates of this position are Boccaccio, Machiavelli, and Galileo, whose works, taken together, show the pervasive influence of secularization on literature, political thought, and science during the early modern period.

BOCCACCIO

Although only a brief time separates Dante's *Divine Comedy* (*ca.* 1307) from Boccaccio's *Decameron* (1348–1353), they portray two fundamentally different views of human nature. Dante's poem centers on the soul's search for salvation and transcendent union with God. Boccaccio's *Decameron* reveals a world in which God's plan and design are no longer clear, and man is left to his own resources to find meaning and purpose in the world. A brief examination of four features of Boccaccio's "human comedy" will bring to light the basic components of the disintegration of the old world and the emergence of the new: the plague of 1348; the principal characters' retreat to the countryside; Fortune, Nature, and Love as the "ministers of the world" controlling the events in the hundred stories; and the key philosophical and theological questions posed in representative stories.[1]

Boccaccio's Introduction to the *Decameron* provides a gripping

---

1. This brief analysis focuses only on questions relating to secularization. There are numerous studies that provide a fuller treatment of Boccaccio's contribution to literature and to the intellectual and cultural developments of his age. One of the best is Judith Serafini-Sauli, *Giovanni Boccaccio* (Boston, 1982).

account of the great plague of 1348, which killed more than one-third of the population of Florence. In the countryside, fields were left untended and crops ready for harvest were left to spoil. In the cities, commerce had come to a virtual standstill. The plague affected more than the material conditions of existence, however; it also tore apart the basic fabric of society. Boccaccio tells us that families left their sick and dying mothers and fathers, brothers and sisters; and priests abandoned their duties to the sick and dying out of fear of contracting the disease. Finally, conditions so deteriorated that there was no one to give the sacraments to the sick and no one to bury the dead in consecrated ground. The plague also shook the foundations of traditional religious belief and raised the most fundamental existential questions about the nature of God and the purpose of existence. At first the plague was thought to be a divine punishment for sin. But it became evident rather quickly that those who led lives of Christian virtue fell victim in far greater numbers than did the opportunists and the rogues who cared only for themselves. In their efforts to minister to the sick and to give proper burial to the dead, the virtuous contracted the disease. Those who avoided their neighbors and even their own families proved more able to avoid the plague. When orthodox practices seemed ineffectual, Boccaccio tells us, many people took up bizarre excesses of asceticism and hedonism.[2]

After this initial description of the ravages of the plague, Boccaccio begins his story with ten characters assembled at the Church of Santa Maria Novella to pray for their friends and loved ones. As they talk they conclude that prayers and other religious acts seem to have no effect. Moreover, by remaining in the city and going into public places such as the church, they increase their risk of contracting the disease. They decide, therefore, to retreat to the countryside. There they propose to feast, enjoy the beauty of nature, and

2. It is worth noting briefly that one of Camus' best-known existential novels uses the plague as a root symbol for the unpredictable, irrational, and capricious forces controlling existence and judges its characters according to their ability to contend with life's ultimate absurdity. His basic contrast is between the priest, who searches for a meaning and justification for the plague in human sin and in God's purpose, and the rebel, who rejects such efforts as "bad faith" and devotes his time and energy to ministering to those who fall victim to the plague.

provide time for the comfort and healing power of friendship and conviviality.

It is important to note that the retreat from the established religious and social structures occurs because they have proven to be ineffective and meaningless. In the new setting, the comfort that the young people yearn for but could not find in the Church is supplied by nature and by friendship. Boccaccio's portrayal of this little community stands in contrast to what conventional society would expect when its constraints are removed. As the young people themselves say, there is no one else at the villa to criticize or to report their behavior to their families and friends. If they were so inclined, they could have given themselves over to debauchery. This does not happen, however, because virtuous behavior, in Boccaccio's view, is neither forced on people by society nor prompted by the desire for some heavenly reward. It is natural to men and women and is the basis for finding meaning and purpose in life.

Of course, not all the characters in the one hundred stories of the *Decameron* behave as honorably as do Boccaccio's principal characters. In fact, the tales seem to offer a catalog of human types from the most wicked to the most virtuous. A pattern emerges from these stories, nevertheless, that suggests the causes of corruption and suffering and of happiness and contentment. In the majority of the stories, human beings are judged by their ability to contend with three existential forces: Fortune, Nature, and Love. A person's greatest assets in dealing with conditions that Fortune and Nature dictate are common sense and quick-wittedness, and the greatest source of comfort and pleasure is love. In this view, virtue or excellence is no longer measured by transcendent or eternal norms and values. Excellence is the ability to survive adversity and to enjoy the pleasures of life while they are available. Although salvation remains an obvious concern, it seems to be ambiguously connected to daily affairs—if at all. Obviously, it is not possible to develop these themes as they unfold in all the stories. We can, however, examine in detail one story that presents the themes that are central to our consideration.

In the opening story, Ciapelletto, "perhaps the worst man ever born," convinces the friar who hears his deathbed confession that he is a saint. Since his character is integral to this story, it is worth quoting Boccaccio's description:

> This Ciapelletto was a man of the following sort: a notary by profession, he would have taken it as a slight upon his honour if one of his legal deeds (and he drew up very few of them) were discovered to be other than false. In fact, he would have drawn up free of charge as many false documents as were requested of him, and done it more willingly than one who was highly paid for his services. He would take great delight in giving false testimony, whether asked for it or not. In those days, great reliance was placed in France upon sworn declarations, and since he had no scruples about swearing falsely, he used to win, by these nefarious means, every case in which he was required to swear upon his faith to tell the truth. He would take particular pleasure, and a great amount of trouble, in stirring up enmity, discord and bad blood between friends, relatives and anybody else; and the more calamities that ensued, the greater would be his rapture. If he were invited to witness a murder or any other criminal act, he would never refuse, but willingly go along; and he often found himself cheerfully assaulting or killing people with his own hands. He was a mighty blasphemer of God and His Saints, losing his temper on the tiniest pretext, as if he were the most hot-blooded man alive. He never went to church, and he would use foul language to pour scorn on all of her sacraments, declaring them repugnant. On the other hand, he would make a point of visiting taverns and other places of ill repute, and supplying them with his custom. . . . But why do I lavish so many words upon him? He was perhaps the worst man ever born.[3]

Ciapelletto is visiting Burgundy on business when he falls deathly ill and his imminent demise puts his hosts in difficult straits. A man on his deathbed is expected to confess his sins. To fail to do so would indicate to the people of Burgundy that Ciapelletto and by implication his hosts were not pious, honest men. On the other hand, Ciapelletto's confession would let the town know that he is a thief and murderer. When his business associates explain their dilemma to him, Ciapelletto offers to give a false confession that will create

---

3. Giovanni Boccaccio, *The Decameron*, trans. G. H. McWilliam (Harmondsworth, Middlesex, 1972), 70f.

the impression that he is a man of great virtue and thereby preserve the (undeserved) good reputation of his hosts. The blasphemy of this act and its damning consequence appear to be of no concern to Ciapelletto. Moreover, his outrageous parody of a confession convinces the naïve friar that he is nothing less than a saint.[4] The friar, persuaded that it would bring great honor to his parish, asks Ciapelletto to allow his body to be buried there. Ciapelletto's clever reply raises an interesting theological issue.

> Yes, father. In fact, I would not wish to be elsewhere, since you have promised that you will pray to God for me. Besides, I have always been especially devoted to your Order. So when you return to your convent, I beg you to see that I am sent that true body of Christ which you consecrate every morning on the altar. For although I am unworthy of it, I intend with your permission to take it, and afterwards to receive the holy Extreme Unction, so that, having lived as a sinner, I shall at least die as a Christian.[5]

Is this last sentence sufficient repentance for Ciapelletto to have gained absolution? Technically, it is an admission of sin and an expression of a yearning to be saved. Has Ciapelletto been able to manipulate dogma and liturgy so that he wins on a technicality? Is God bound by this quick-witted but perhaps halfhearted confession?

While the text does not respond directly to these questions, it does report that Ciapelletto's fame as a pious and holy man grew to such proportions that people began to call him Saint Ciapelletto. "Moreover it is claimed that through him God has wrought many miracles, and that He continues to work them on behalf of whoever commends himself devoutly to this particular Saint."[6] In other tales, Boccaccio uses similar circumstances to ridicule the gullibility of

4. When the friar asks him if he had ever borne false witness against any man, or spoken ill of people, or taken what belonged to others without seeking their permission, Ciapelletto replies that he did on one occasion speak ill of someone. He once had a neighbor who was forever beating his wife, and so on one occasion he spoke ill of him to his wife's kinfolk, for he felt extremely sorry for that unfortunate woman. Ciapelletto also confesses that once, without thinking what he was doing, he spat in the house of God. The friar reassures him that there is nothing to worry about because he and the members of the clergy spit there continually. Ciapelletto is appalled to learn this and severely rebukes the friar. Boccaccio, *Decameron*, 76f.

5. *Ibid.*, 79.
6. *Ibid.*, 81.

ignorant believers, but he is clearly not doing so here.[7] Those who pray to God through Ciapelletto have their prayers answered and miracles are performed. The storyteller comments that God often manipulates human plans and purposes in ways incomprehensible to man because "the human eye [is] . . . quite unable to penetrate the secrets of divine intelligence." The point is made again in the final paragraph of the story:

> Nor would I wish to deny that perhaps God has blessed and admitted him to His presence. For albeit he led a wicked, sinful life, it is possible that at the eleventh hour he was so sincerely repentant that God had mercy upon him and received him into His kingdom. But since this is hidden from us, I speak only with regard to the outward appearance, and I say that this fellow should rather be in Hell, in the hands of the devil, than in Paradise. And if this is the case, we may recognize how very great is God's loving kindness towards us, in that it takes account, not of our error, but of the purity of our faith, and grants our prayers even when we appoint as our emissary one who is His enemy, thinking him to be His friend, as though we were appealing to one who was truly holy as our intercessor for His favour.[8]

That Boccaccio uses this as the opening story in his "human comedy" is highly significant. First of all, the narrator repeatedly states that salvation and damnation seem to be matters that are mysterious and ultimately unknowable. Second, there is a repeated questioning of man's ability to see things in proper perspective.[9]

7. The most famous example is the tale of Cipolla (Day 6, Story 10), who tells a crowd of country folk that he has brought back from his pilgrimage "one of the holes from the Holy Cross, and a small phial containing some of the sound from the bells of Solomon's temple" (512) and the coals from the martyrdom of Saint Lawrence, which, for a contribution, he will use to mark the sign of the cross on the heads of the people and guarantee that "for a whole year they will never be touched by fire without getting burnt" (Boccaccio, *Decameron*, 513).

8. *Ibid.*, 69, 81.

9. Several other stories develop the key theme of appearance versus reality. Contrary to Dante's urging to see beyond the surface to reality, Boccaccio's characters demonstrate that—at least on the human plane—appearance is reality. Two famous stories that present this theme are those of Alatiel (Day 2, Story 7), who, "despite the fact that eight separate men had made love to her on thousands of different occasions, . . . entered [her husband's] bed as a virgin and convinced him that it was really so," and Masetto (Day 3, Story 1), who, despite his lecherous behavior with several convent nuns, devised a plan that not only made his own life comfortable but also convinced the people in the village that the nuns' virtue and devotion were responsible for miracles (240ff.).

Third, the story raises fundamental questions about the Church as God's instrument of salvation.

This story provides an excellent illustration of the theme of secularization because it shows how the bond between the sacred and the secular has disintegrated. The sacred does not disappear; there is still concern for salvation, but salvation seems to have little to do with everyday life. Moreover, God's plan and purpose for the world and his use of human actions are not readily apparent to man. Therefore, all that man can do is trust his eternal destiny to God and concentrate on living his life in a way that brings as much pleasure and satisfaction as possible. Most of the other tales do not have characters as villainous as Ciapelletto. Numerous times, however, the stories make it clear that fortune or misfortune has little to do with ethical conduct or good intentions. In fact, the virtuous often suffer the most.[10]

It should be noted, however, that the *Decameron* is not pessimistic or cynical about the human condition. Boccaccio affirms the intrinsic value of secular existence. Nature can alleviate suffering and nourish the human spirit; companionship and love ease pain, bring joy, and dignify life.

MACHIAVELLI

Machiavelli also finds that the catastrophes of his time have shaken the foundations of conventional views of human nature and society. It is not the plague, however, that is ravaging Machiavelli's world; it is political turmoil and upheaval that have weakened Florence and the rest of the Italian city-states. For Machiavelli, the only hope for his city and his country lies in the emergence of a political leader who is not encumbered by outmoded notions of virtue and is, therefore, capable of taking decisive action to restore and maintain political order.[11]

10. The most famous example is the story of Griselda (Day 10, Story 10).

11. This examination of Machiavelli, like that of Boccaccio, concentrates on the theme of secularization and does not attempt to consider the many other dimensions of his writings or the pertinent scholarship on it. Also, this analysis attempts to point to elements of Machiavelli that have not received the attention they deserve. For a helpful discussion of such well-established themes in Machiavelli as his attacks on Christianity, Christian theology, and the Platonic concept of politics, see Leo Strauss, *Thoughts on Machiavelli* (Seattle, 1969).

In the *Prince*, Machiavelli urges the ruler to recognize that Fortune and Necessity rather than divine providence set the conditions under which man must live.[12] The standards for measuring human excellence or virtue, therefore, are quite different from those of classical philosophy or Christian theology. It is this revised conception of virtue that most clearly demonstrates how his view of human nature departs from the medieval description.

One of the primary subjects of medieval iconography is the depiction of the psychomachia, the battle in the soul between virtue and vice. These iconic representations are an amalgamation of ideas from classical philosophy and Christian theology.[13] The concept of a psychomachia expresses the basic Platonic notion of the soul as the site of the struggle between human reason and appetite. The most memorable presentation occurs in the *Phaedrus:* the soul is like a charioteer who has to steer two powerful horses pulling in opposite directions. The horses are the appetites and noetic reason, *i.e.*, the human capacity to see within the physical world the intimations of absolute beauty and truth. Medieval theology combined the four Platonic virtues (temperance, fortitude, prudence, and justice) with three theological virtues (faith, hope, and charity). The seven were frequently depicted as rungs on a ladder that carried man from the material to the spiritual or, more broadly, from the secular to the sacred. Machiavelli, however, sets up only one cardinal virtue— the ability to survive, which he associates principally with military cunning. In his reconceptualization, Machiavelli transforms conventional virtues into the hollow means of creating a public image. A prince should, for example, give the appearance of generosity but not be foolish enough to be generous. Or he should try to gain the affection of his subjects, but should realize that being feared is more important than being loved. While public appearance is important, the ultimate factors determining the behavior of the prince should be survival and expediency. If deceit, theft, and murder are re-

12. For references to detailed discussions of Fortune and Necessity in Machiavelli's works, see *The Prince*, edited and translated with introduction and annotation by James B. Atkinson (Indianapolis, 1976), which has an excellent bibliography.

13. For a discussion of the psychomachia and its treatment in medieval iconography, see Emile Male, *The Gothic Image: Religious Art in France of the Thirteenth Century*, trans. Dora Nussey (New York, 1958).

quired, these actions should be taken and taken without hesitation and with a clear conscience.

Although Machiavelli's redefinition of virtue is regarded as a Renaissance innovation, it actually represents a return to the view found in the Homeric epics. In the *Iliad* and the *Odyssey*, Ulysses is the hero who most displays excellence (*aretē*) by using military cunning to defeat his adversaries. The intent of Machiavelli's revival of the warrior's *virtue* becomes clearer when compared to the later philosophical concept that is adopted by medieval thinkers. In classical philosophy, excellence becomes associated with the Platonic ordering of the soul; excellence is right action guided by reason.[14] Machiavelli's redefinition of virtue as military cunning is a deliberate rejection of this classical conception of the soul as the site of the union between man and the transcendent source of truth and justice.[15] This reconception is augmented by his revision of the standard Renaissance interpretation of Chiron the centaur as an allegorical depiction of man dominated by his animalic nature.

A standard motif in classical iconography is the battle of the Lapiths and the centaurs. The Lapiths, as the legendary founders of Greece, represent rational man and the centaurs, nonrational, barbarian man. The Renaissance's iconographic interest in the centaur centered on Chiron, who taught the Greeks the use of archery, which gave them superiority in warfare. In Renaissance art Chiron is portrayed as a melancholy figure because he realizes that he can never be fully human. Depicted this way, Chiron stands as a symbol of the struggle between the powerful forces of appetite and reason within the soul. Man's basic yearning is to follow the lead of reason, but what thwarts this striving is the counterpull of appetite and

14. Two classic studies that trace this key development in detail are Bruno Snell, *The Discovery of the Mind: The Greek Origins of European Thought*, trans. T. G. Rosenmeyer (Cambridge, Mass., 1953), translation of *Die Entdeckung des Geistes: Studien zur Entstehung des europäischen Denkens bei den Griechen* (2nd ed.; Hamburg, 1948); and Hermann Frankel, *Early Greek Poetry and Philosophy: A History of Greek Epic, Lyric, and Prose to the Middle of the Fifth Century* (New York, 1973). See also Walter Otto, *The Homeric Gods: The Spiritual Significance of Greek Religion*, trans. Moses Hadas (New York, 1954), for a discussion of the corresponding transformation of Athena from the warrior-goddess of epic poetry to the goddess of wisdom in tragedy and philosophy.

15. He is also rejecting the famous Platonic definition of politics—'man writ large'—in which the well-ordered soul serves as the model for political order.

instinct.[16] Machiavelli ignores this emphasis on Chiron's melancholy and presents him as an ideal figure for the prince to emulate. The centaur is the ideal warrior because his animal cunning and ruthlessness are not hindered by "reason" or by abstract notions of justice or goodness. Precisely because he is not encumbered by such inhibiting concerns, the centaur is better prepared to subdue Fortune, gain power, and achieve fame. So, here again, Machiavelli turns a conventional motif upside down to show his rejection of traditional views of human nature.[17]

His position clearly represents a more radical form of secularization than does Boccaccio's. In Machiavelli's writings, the sacred side of the human soul disappears and only the secular elements, *i.e.*, appetite, instinct, and emotion, remain. In the most virtuous men, these animalic qualities are guided by intelligence, but it is an intelligence associated with military cunning and not with philosophical or theological reason. Moreover, Machiavelli's more radical secularization is evident in his view that religion is significant only as a potential source of political order or disorder. It is useful if it inspires a people to serve the state; it is a threat if it undercuts loyalty to the state. Similarly, Machiavelli has little or nothing to say about man's salvation or about God's role in secular affairs. In his secular view, there is little or no concern with life beyond the here and now; and man, not God, is responsible for giving existence its meaning and purpose.[18]

If we reflect briefly on the discussion of both Machiavelli and Boccaccio, we see that reason, which is crucial to the theological and philosophical view of human nature, is given little significance. This is because reason is directly related to the belief in an orderly, intel-

16. Botticelli's *Minerva and the Centaur* is an excellent example of this motif.

17. Machiavelli, *The Prince*, Chap. 18, pp. 279ff. In the same section, Machiavelli also urges the prince to develop the attributes of the lion (violence) and the fox (fraud). In Dante's *Inferno*, falling victim to the habits of the lion and the leopard (his symbol for fraud) leads to damnation.

18. For additional discussions of secularization in Machiavelli, see Hans Baron, "Secularization of Wisdom and Political Humanism in the Renaissance," *Journal of the History of Ideas*, XXI (1960), 131–50; and J. A. Mazzeo, *Renaissance and Seventeenth Century Studies* (New York, 1964), 90–165; and Mazzeo, *Renaissance and Revolution: The Remaking of European Thought* (New York, 1965), 69–130.

ligible world. In Boccaccio and Machiavelli, the well-ordered, providentially guided world disappears and, as a result, so does the human capacity to comprehend it. Reason becomes insignificant because it is associated with the yearning for the transcendent, divine source of beauty and truth. In Boccaccio, there is a gulf between human understanding and God's actions in the world. In Machiavelli, the transcendent ground of being is nonexistent; therefore, reason also disappears and is replaced by prudent planning and military cunning.

GALILEO

Galileo does not share Boccaccio's and Machiavelli's conviction that the world is irrational and reason is therefore irrelevant. Nevertheless, Galileo's concept of reason is very different from that of medieval theology. For the scholastics, reason is the beginning of the questioning and probing that prepares the soul for the revelation of divine truth. For Galileo, reason is associated with experimentation, observation, and induction, *viz.*, the scientific method.

As this controversy between science and religion mounts, Galileo attempts to distinguish the subject and method of the two fields of knowledge. A key document in this regard is his "Letter to the Grand Duchess Christina." Although it is addressed to a member of the Medici family, the intended audience is actually ecclesiastical authorities in Rome who are being pressured to bring charges of heresy against him.[19] In attempting to demonstrate that his work is not heretical, Galileo carefully steers his argument from generally accepted theological propositions to his own controversial views. Unfortunately, we cannot follow his entire argument.[20] Instead, we will join it where he attempts to point out the difficulties with scriptural interpretation, for it is here that he presents the case for a

19. See Stillman Drake's useful introduction and translation in *Discoveries and Opinions of Galileo* (Garden City, N.Y., 1957).
20. This analysis focuses on the specific topic of secularization and does not attempt to deal with other dimensions of Galileo's work. It should also be noted that not all elements of his work are this starkly secular. Some even reflect Neoplatonic immanentization. The thrust of the analysis offered here, however, fits with the general view of Galileo. Moreover, his use of Platonic concepts leads to results very different from those achieved by Ficino, Pico, and other religious magi.

revised understanding of the role of theology as queen of the sciences.

> [I]t is very pious to say and prudent to affirm that the holy Bible can never speak untruth—whenever its true meaning is understood. But I believe nobody will deny that it is often very abstruse, and may say things which are quite different from what its bare words signify. Hence in expounding the Bible if one were always to confine oneself to the unadorned grammatical meaning, one might fall into error. Not only contradictions and propositions far from true might thus be made to appear in the Bible, but even grave heresies and follies. Thus it would be necessary to assign to God feet, hands, and eyes, as well as corporeal and human affections, such as anger, repentance, hatred, and sometimes even the forgetting of things past and ignorance of those to come.[21]

Galileo then turns to the question of why passages in the Scriptures are ambiguous and abstruse. The explanation is that "these propositions uttered by the Holy Ghost were set down in that manner by the sacred scribes in order to accommodate them to the capacities of the common people, who were rude and unlearned. . . . The rule has been observed of avoiding confusion in the minds of the common people which would render them contumacious toward the higher mysteries." This principle, Galileo argues, is especially applicable to the biblical description of the physical world.

> Now the Bible, merely to condescend to popular capacity, has not hesitated to obscure some very important pronouncements, attributing to God himself some qualities extremely remote from (and even contrary to) His essence. Who, then, would positively declare that this principle has been set aside, and the Bible has confined itself rigorously to the bare and restricted sense of its words, when speaking but casually of the earth, of water, of the sun, or of any other created thing? Especially in view of the fact that these things in no way concern the primary purpose of the sacred writings, which is the service of God and the salvation of souls—matters infinitely beyond the comprehension of the common people.[22]

21. Galileo Galilei, "Letter to the Grand Duchess Christina," in *Discoveries*, 181.
22. *Ibid.*, 182.

This is a very clever argument. Theologians have themselves conceded that the Bible has had to describe God in ways that common people can understand. Galileo, in turn, contends that the Bible does not take the trouble to be scientifically accurate in describing natural phenomena because that would confuse the ignorant and could become a distraction. Moreover, its references to the natural world are incidental to its primary purpose—the salvation of the soul. Galileo then moves to one of his central arguments.

> This being granted, I think that in discussions of physical problems we ought to begin not from the authority of scriptural passages, but from sense-experiences and necessary demonstrations. . . . It is necessary for the Bible, in order to be accommodated to the understanding of every man, to speak many things which appear to differ from the absolute truth. . . . But Nature, on the other hand, is inexorable and immutable; she never transgresses the laws imposed upon her, or cares a wit whether her abstruse reasons and methods of operation are understandable to men. For that reason it appears that nothing physical which sense-experience sets before our eyes, or which necessary demonstrations prove to us, ought to be called in question (much less condemned) upon the testimony of biblical passages which may have some different meaning beneath their words.

Realizing that he is venturing into dangerous territory, Galileo hastens to indicate that his intent is not to compromise the majesty or the authority of the Scriptures. The basic subject of the Scriptures is the salvation of souls, and in these matters "the Bible was designed to persuade men of those articles and propositions which, surpassing all human reasoning, could not be made credible by science, or by any other means than through the very mouth of the Holy Spirit." This is a prudent affirmation on Galileo's part, but it also serves to limit the authority of Scripture to the fundamental matter of salvation.

> From these things it follows as a necessary consequence that, since the Holy Ghost did not intend to teach us whether heaven moves or stands still, whether its shape is spherical or like a discus or extended in a plane, nor whether the earth is located at its center or off to one side, then so much the less was it intended to settle for us any other conclusion of the same kind. . . . Now if the Holy Spirit has purposely

neglected to teach us propositions of this sort as irrelevant to the highest goal (that is, to our salvation), how can anyone affirm that it is obligatory to take sides on them, and that one belief is required by faith, while the other side is erroneous? Can an opinion be heretical and yet have no concern with the salvation of souls? . . . I would say here something that was heard from an ecclesiastic of the most eminent degree: "That the intention of the Holy Ghost is to teach us how one goes to heaven, not how heaven goes."[23]

We have now arrived at the fundamental point that Galileo wishes to make: a clarification of theology's role.

[Some theologians] say that since theology is queen of all the sciences, she need not bend in any way to accommodate herself to the teachings of less worthy sciences which are subordinate to her; these others must rather be referred to her as to their supreme empress, changing and altering their conclusions according to her statutes and decrees. They add further that if in the inferior sciences any conclusion should be taken as certain in virtue of demonstrations or experiences, while in the Bible another conclusion is found repugnant to this, then the professors of that science should themselves undertake to undo their proofs and discover the fallacies in their own experiences, without bothering the theologians and exegetes. For, they say, it does not become the dignity of theology to stoop to the investigation of fallacies in the subordinate sciences; it is sufficient for her merely to determine the truth of a given conclusion with absolute authority, secure in her inability to err.

Galileo is, of course, describing the scholastic view of theology. The explanation of all that exists is ultimately derived from an understanding of God's will and purpose. Therefore, any field of inquiry from natural philosophy to ethics is but a subfield of theology and must always be subject to its principles and authority. Galileo offers another explanation. "[Theology] might deserve that name by reason of including everything that is learned from all the other sciences and establishing everything by better methods and with profounder learning. . . . Or theology might be queen because of being occupied with a subject which excels in dignity all the subjects

23. Ibid., 182f., 185f.

which compose the other sciences, and because her teachings are divulged in more sublime ways." Of these two possibilities, Galileo maintains that the latter is correct. "[No theologian], I think, will say that geometry, astronomy, music, and medicine are much more excellently contained in the Bible than they are in the books of Archimedes, Ptolemy, Boethius, and Galen. Hence it seems likely that regal pre-eminence is given to theology in the second sense; that is, by reason of its subject and the miraculous communication of divine revelation of conclusions which could not be conceived by men in any other way, concerning chiefly the attainment of eternal blessedness."[24]

Here in concise form Galileo has set out a fundamental feature of secularization. Theology's reign is restricted to knowledge of salvation. The other areas of inquiry that had been subject to her rule are now autonomous fields with their own epistemological principles. By implication, Galileo is also revising the long-standing view of reason and its relation to revelation. In scholastic theology, reason's function is to initiate the search for salvation. Galileo removes reason's religious function and establishes it as an autonomous mode of inquiry whose aim is to understand the physical world—to understand how the heavens go, not how to go to Heaven.

Numerous other texts could be used to develop further dimensions of the pattern of secularization. These three, however, are sufficient to set the main lines and suggest something of the range of issues involved. They illustrate the basic break in the relationship of the secular and the sacred and show how emphasis on *saeculum* affects the understanding of human nature, society, the world, and God. Human nature is assessed in terms of physical and emotional needs and is measured by the ability to use common sense and opportunity to forestall misfortune and to capitalize on good fortune. Society is no longer a microcosm of the divine macrocosm. Social and political order and disorder ebb and flow as the cycle of Fortune turns, and human appetites and longings serve as the basis both for social and political upheaval and for efforts at stability. The natural world also gains independence from divine providence. It is

24. *Ibid.*, 191ff.

either controlled by Fortune and Necessity, as in the work of Boccaccio and Machiavelli, or it is a self-contained system indifferent to man, as in Galileo. God is either remote from this world and human affairs or is dismissed altogether as irrelevant.

THE ORIGINS OF THE SACRALIZING PATTERN IN THE RENAISSANCE

While secularization minimizes or altogether dismisses the sacred, the process of sacralization obliterates the categorical distinctions so that the secular becomes indistinguishable from the sacred. The process also produces profound changes in the traditional medieval view of human nature: man loses his creaturely limitations and becomes a terrestrial god capable of creating an earthly Paradise.

The source for this sacralizing process is the Ancient Wisdom tradition, particularly the Hermetic writings. While philological studies as early as the seventeenth century made it clear that the Hermetic writings belong to the late Hellenistic period, Ficino and the Neoplatonists believed them to be the earliest and the most complete accounts of the revelations God provided prior to the Christian Gospels.[25] Some Neoplatonists even believed that Hermes Trismegistus was the teacher of both Moses and Plato and looked to his teaching as a means of reestablishing the essential core of God's revelation and as a means for guiding the union of Christian theology with Greek philosophy.

Ficino and the members of the Platonic Academy were particularly drawn to those elements of the Hermetic tradition that seem to provide the basis for a new (or renewed) understanding of human nature. A key text in this regard is the section of the *Poimandres* or *Pimander* known as the "Egyptian Genesis."[26]

As the account opens, Hermes is deeply troubled by his inability

25. Casaubon in 1614 supplied the philological evidence that showed that the Hermetic Corpus was from Hellenistic times.

26. The standard edition of the *Corpus Hermeticum* was prepared by A. D. Nock and A. J. Festugière and published by Guillaume. Volume I, covering Books I–XII (the *Poimandres*), appeared in 1945, and Volume II, covering Books XIII–XVIII (the *Asclepius*), appeared in 1954. An edition with an introduction, notes, and an English translation is also found in *Hermetica*, ed. Walter Scott (4 vols.; 1924–36; rpr. London, 1968). The principal analysis of these materials is found in Festugière, *La Révélation*.

to understand the meaning of existence and is further confused by
the learned ignorance of the theologians. After he falls into a deep
sleep, the divine messenger Pimander appears and indicates that
God has sent him to answer the existential questions troubling
Hermes. When Hermes expresses his desire to know the true nature
of man and the world, Pimander begins with the *true* account of
creation. The supreme God and the divine Father of mankind instructed the Demiurge to create the natural world. Man, however, is
created directly by the divine Father and in His image. Man, therefore, is beautiful and shares in the creative powers of divinity. When
primal man viewed the creation being fashioned by the Demiurge,
he yearned to use his own creative powers and obtained permission
from the Father to assist the Demiurge. The Demiurge, who loves
this son of God, teaches him the essential nature of the created
order; and man is thereby able to participate in the creation.

> And he [man] who had full power over the world of things mortal
> and over the irrational animals . . . having broken through the
> [celestial] vault showed to lower Nature the beautiful form of God.
> When [Nature] beheld him who had in himself inexhaustible beauty
> and all the forces of the Governors combined with the form of God,
> she smiled in love; for she had seen the reflection of this most beau-
> tiful form of Man in the water and its shadow upon the earth. He too,
> seeing his likeness present in her, reflected in the water, loved it and
> desired to dwell in it. At once with the wish it become reality, and he
> came to inhabit the form devoid of reason. And Nature, having re-
> ceived into herself the beloved, embraced him wholly and they
> mingled: for they were inflamed with love. And this is why alone of
> all the animals on earth man is twofold, mortal through the body,
> immortal through the essential Man.[27]

Several important features emerge from this compact myth. First
of all, man's exalted role in relation to creation and to all other beings
is emphasized. Primal man joins the creative hierarchy by receiving
creative power from God and combining it with the Demiurge's

27. *Corpus Hermeticum*, I, 13. This translation is found in Jonas, *The Gnostic Religion*, 150f. The Jonas translation is generally more literal than Scott's is.

knowledge of the cosmos. Man's special relation to God is underscored by the repeated references to their Father-son relationship.
Second, subordinate deities (the Demiurge and the Celestial Gover-
nors) and the creation (Nature) adore man and willingly yield to
him. Third, the myth offers an immanentist view of the relation of
man's spiritual and physical natures (spiritual man sees his reflection in Nature; Nature recognizes man's divinity). This conception,
of course, stands in contrast to the dualistic view in which the physical world is an impediment or a trap preventing man from realizing
his divinity. As we shall see, Ficino embellishes this immanentist
view to the point that man's physical nature is made a necessary
condition for the exercise of his divine creativity.

The second major book of the Hermetic Corpus, the *Asclepius*,
also provides a revelation of man's true nature. It opens with an
exalted view of man similar to that found in the "Egyptian Genesis."
Then Hermes, who is conveying what he has learned through divine revelation, explains that "what we have said about man is
already marvellous, but most marvellous of all is that he has been
able to discover the nature of the gods and to reproduce it. . . . [The
magi] mingled a virtue, drawn from material nature, to the substance of the statues, and . . . evoked the souls of demons or angels
into their idols."[28] This magical power enables man to participate in
the maintenance of cosmic order and to create a microcosmic social
order. But if this is man's true nature and the true relation of the
cosmos to God and man, why is there such a profound existential
ignorance and why has man so thoroughly forgotten his role as
magus? The *Asclepius* does not offer an explanation but does reas-
sure mankind that the current confusion will be overcome (through
the teachings of Hermes) and mankind will thereby attain its full
humanity. When man realizes his true nature, it will be possible to
restore the world to its first beauty so that it will again be worthy of
reverence and admiration.

The Hermetic view of man as magus, as God's designated emis-
sary appointed to maintain the macrocosm and to perfect the micro-

28. *Corpus Hermeticum*, II, 347f. This translation is from Yates, *Giordano Bruno*, 37.

cosm, is further developed in *Picatrix*, a textbook of magical procedures.[29] The fourth book's discussion of talismans and images also offers an account of the marvelous city of Adocentyn, which was founded and governed by the supreme magus, Hermes Trismegistus.

> There are among the Chaldeans very perfect masters in this art [making magic images] and they affirm that Hermes was the first who constructed images by means of which he knew how to regulate the Nile against the motion of the moon. This man also built a temple to the Sun. . . . It was he, too, who in the east of Egypt constructed a City . . . within which he constructed a castle which had four gates in each of its four parts. . . . [H]e introduced spirits [into the images guarding each gate] which spoke with voices, nor could anyone enter the gates of the City except by their permission. There he planted trees in the midst of which was a great tree which bore the fruit of all generation. . . . Near the City there was abundance of waters in which dwelt many kinds of fish. Around the circumference of the City he placed engraved images and ordered them in such a manner that by their virtue the inhabitants were made virtuous and withdrawn from all wickedness and harm.[30]

This mythic utopia represents the fulfillment of Hermes' assurance that the time of troubles mentioned in the *Asclepius* could be overcome. According to this text, Hermes used the knowledge made available to him to establish a perfect social order operating in harmony with the divine cosmos. In this brief passage, we find that man first controls those events in nature that adversely affect him, for example, the flooding of the Nile. The second creative act is to use the knowledge of the natural order to produce an abundant supply of food to meet man's physical needs. The third is to protect the inhabitants of the city from external threats. It is the final act, however, that is truly extraordinary. By manipulating the influence of astral powers, the legislator-priest is able to make the city's inhabitants virtuous.

---

29. The *Picatrix* is not attributed directly to Hermes Trismegistus, though it refers to him as one of the greatest magi. The text reached Europe in an Arabic edition and was a basic source for Ficino's understanding of magic and Hermetism.

30. *Picatrix*, Bk. IV, Chap. 3. This text is taken from Yates, *Giordano Bruno*, 54.

These mythic accounts of man's creation and his role in the world obviously differ markedly from those found in the biblical Genesis. The most striking contrast is in the emphasis on knowledge. In Genesis 3, for example, man is punished for attempting to eat of the Tree of Knowledge (and the Tree of Life) so that he could be like God. For this sin, man is driven from Eden and punished not only with physical suffering but also by a profound rupture in his union with God. This theme of divine knowledge being forbidden to man is also a central element in the story of the Tower of Babel. In this myth, man decides to build a tower so he can storm the heavens and occupy the place of God. To confound man's attempt to overstep his boundaries in such a defiant way, God disrupts his ability to communicate. By contrast, the Hermetic myths underscore man's divinity and describe man as possessing both God-like knowledge and the creative capacity to use that knowledge to emulate God's creation. Rather than forbidding man to have God-like knowledge and powers, the Hermetic myths present them as the Father's gifts to his son.

While it is significant for our purposes to demonstrate the basic differences between this sacralizing pattern and the Judaeo-Christian tradition, it is also important to indicate again that Ficino and the Neoplatonists did not find pronounced conflicts between the Hermetic materials and Christianity. For Ficino, the apparent conflicts in the various ancient revelations were to be reconciled by establishing the essential core common to all the texts.[31]

The immanentizing emphasis of the Hermetic materials, however, stands in contrast to the radically dualistic views of other esoteric religions and especially to Gnosticism. Since one of the primary modes of interpreting modernity develops parallels with Gnosticism, it is important to examine the principal differences between it and Hermetism, which plays such a prominent role in the sacralizing tradition. The basic differences between the Hermetic and the Gnostic views and their significance for interpreting mod-

31. In subsequent generations, fundamental differences between Church dogma and the newly recovered Ancient Wisdom do become significant. Agrippa, Bruno, and Campanella become convinced that these materials are superior to the traditional Christian Scriptures.

ernity can be developed through a brief examination of one of the classic Gnostic texts, "The Hymn of the Pearl." This text opens:

> When I was a little child and dwelt in the kingdom of my Father's house and delighted in the wealth and splendor of those who raised me, my parents sent me forth from the East, our homeland, with provisions for the journey. From the riches of our treasure-house they tied me a burden: great it was, yet light, so that I might carry it alone. . . . They took off from me the robe of glory which in their love they had made for me, and my purple mantle that was woven to conform exactly to my figure, and made a covenant with me, and wrote it in my heart that I might not forget it: "When thou goest down into Egypt and bringest the One Pearl which lies in the middle of the sea which is encircled by the snorting serpent, thou shalt put on again thy robe of glory and thy mantle over it and with thy brother our next in rank be heir in our kingdom."

While in Egypt, the narrator meets "one of my race" who warns against the Egyptians and "contact with the unclean ones." The Egyptians nevertheless "ingratiated themselves with me, and mixed me [drink] with their cunning, and gave me to taste of their meat; and I forgot that I was a king's son and served their king. I forgot the Pearl for which my parents had sent me. Through the heaviness of their nourishment I sank into deep slumber." This "ingratiation" is a trap the Egyptians deliberately spring on the royal visitor. The son's predicament causes great anxiety in his father's kingdom, and it is decided that a letter will be prepared and sent to the son in the hope that it will remind him of his real identity.

> From thy father the King of Kings, and from thy mother, mistress of the East, and from thy brother, our next in rank, unto thee, our son in Egypt, greeting. Awake and rise up out of thy sleep, and perceive the words of our letter. Remember that thou art a king's son: behold whom thou hast served in bondage. Be mindful of the Pearl, for whose sake thou hast departed into Egypt. Remember thy robe of glory, recall thy splendid mantle, that thou mayest put them on and deck thyself with them and thy name be read in the book of the heroes and thou become with thy brother, our deputy, heir in our kingdom.[32]

32. This text appears in Jonas, *The Gnostic Religion*, 113–14.

The message is given over to an eagle who is capable of avoiding "the children of Babel and the rebellious demons of Sarbûg." Upon receipt of the message, the son remembers his royal origin and awakens from his slumber. Immediately he sets out to "enchant the terrible and snorting serpent," recover the pearl, and return to his father's kingdom. "Their filthy and impure garment I put off, and left it behind in their land, and directed my way that I might come to the light of our homeland, the East."[33] The son completes his mission, and there is much joy that the pearl is returned and that the son is safely home.

Even if the specific Gnostic meaning of certain symbols is not known, the thrust of this myth is clear and its contrast to the Hermetic myths evident. The king of kings is the supreme God, and the son of God who is sent to Egypt is comparable to primal man in the Hermetic myth. In attempting to recover the pearl, the son becomes trapped in matter and forgets his divine origin and mission. The pessimistic, dualistic view of the physical is expressed in references to food and drink as the source of trickery, the garments (worn to be like the Egyptians) as filthy, and the consequences of the treachery as slumber and sleepwalking. The eagle is a universal symbol of a divine messenger. The meaning of the pearl is perhaps not so readily apparent, though myths of a great treasure lost in the dross of the world are a frequent component of dualistic religions. Most often it refers to the soul that becomes imprisoned in matter and has to be rescued by divine action. This is the meaning here. Without explaining how the divine soul becomes entrapped, the myth nevertheless expresses this fundamental condition. The effects of the material world are so strong that even God's son forgets his true nature and his real home.

This hymn is regarded as Gnostic because of its emphasis on knowledge (*gnosis*) as the means of salvation. This feature is also found, however, in the Hermetic myths' doctrine that knowledge enables man to achieve his fulfillment as the Son of God. Fundamental differences exist, however, in the two views of what constitutes salvation through knowledge. In the Gnostic myth, salvation, *i.e.,*

33. *Ibid.*, 115.

regaining one's divine station, depends on escaping from the world. In the Hermetic myth, the world is necessary for mankind to exercise his divine creativity, and it is there that man builds the social microcosm that completes creation.

Given the fundamental Gnostic doctrines of the world as a prison and of *gnosis* as producing salvation through liberation from the physical world, it is difficult to understand how Gnostic myths can be equated with modern programs of social reformation. On the other hand, the Hermetic myths and symbols have a close correspondence to modern dreams of innerworldly fulfillment. The Hermetic materials present man as magus, who possesses God-like knowledge to master nature and to perfect society.

It is because of this emphasis on man's divinization that the term *sacralization* is used to characterize the impact of these materials on Renaissance and modern views of human nature and society. In the *prisci theologi* tradition, the secular, material world is the locus of the fulfillment of the salvation story. Moreover, the choice of the term *sacralization* is consistent with Neoplatonic terminology. Ficino, as we shall see, refers to "divinization" in his new philosophy, and this is equivalent to *sacralization*.

With this analysis of the sacralizing tradition, it is now possible to show clearly how this process contrasts with secularization and how it relates to modern thought and experience. Secularization breaks apart the tension between the sacred and the secular. As the brief treatment of Boccaccio, Machiavelli, and Galileo demonstrates, the role of the sacred is greatly diminished or is eliminated altogether from secular affairs. In the concept of man that emerges, the appetites and instrumental reason become the sources of understanding and explaining individual and social behavior and aspirations. The "higher" elements of man's nature, supposedly derived from his divine nature, are minimized or dismissed. In the secular view, the natural world is governed by forces that are indifferent to mankind, and virtue and dignity are measured by the ability to master Fortune.

By contrast, the sacralizing process divinizes the secular, transforming it to the point that only the sacred is retained. In this conception, man's essential nature is divine. His natural instincts and appetites, if they exist at all, are aids to his knowledge of the world. They serve his highest intellectual capacities, which are boundless and equal to God's. He not only knows and understands the natural world; he can control it and shape it to his purposes. The divine, rather than being remote from the world, is immanent in it, working with man to complete the creation and perfect human existence. Nature is not indifferent to man. The powers that control nature are co-creators with man, and man may even be their superior. At any rate, nature provides man comfort and happiness and, more important, is the means of expressing his fundamental creativity.

These myths, it should be noted, open new perspectives on the origins of features of modernity analyzed by Löwith and Voegelin. Both find in modern epochal consciousness a conception of inner-worldly fulfillment accomplished by man; and each finds the core of modernity in the doctrine of salvation through knowledge and the view of man as the new master of history. The difficulty is that these formulations rest upon the notion that a radically transcendent religious world view, Christianity or Gnosticism, has been transformed into an innerworldly one. Critics have, in turn, questioned the legitimacy of this explanation and have challenged its proponents to document the stages at which such a profound transformation can be shown to occur. This study shows that the source of this pattern in modernity is found in the immanentist, sacralizing myths of the Ancient Wisdom tradition. The key point of assimilation and transmission of this tradition is Ficino and the Platonic Academy.

Chapter Three

FICINO, PICO, AND THE NEW GOD: ANTHROPOS

In his dedicatory preface, Ficino explains that one of the primary purposes of the *Theologica Platonica* is "to present a new understanding of human nature." His principal contention is that man is the most extraordinary of God's creatures because of the unique union of the spiritual and the physical in his soul. Proper understanding of the soul's structure enables man to draw upon the spiritual element to overcome his physical limitations and to escape Fate. This process of spiritualization transforms man from a determined creature like all others into the greatest of God's miracles—a terrestrial god. In the *De vita triplici*, Ficino argues that astral magic is the highest form of natural philosophy and explains how the magus can draw upon the celestial powers to become like God in knowledge and creative ability.[1]

Pico's *Oration on Human Dignity* also presents a new view of human nature and introduces magic as the highest form of knowl-

1. The *Theologia Platonica de Immortalitatie Animarium* was written between 1469 and 1474 and was printed in 1482; the *De vita triplici*, or *De Vita Libre Tres*, was published in 1489. These texts appear in Marsilio Ficino, *Opera Omnia* (4 vols.; Basel, 1561, 1576). The second edition was reprinted in Torino in 1959 by Bottega d'Erasmo. This edition, which is cited in this study, contains an introduction by P. O. Kristeller and a foreword (*premessa*) by Mario Sancipriano.

edge.[2] This text is important for understanding the influence of sacralization on modern thought for two reasons. First of all, Pico presents a new myth of the creation of man and of man's relation to God. This remythologizing provides a convenient point of comparison with the Hermetic myth and with modern epochal consciousness. Second, this text has long stood as one of the most celebrated examples of the epochal break with the theological "dark ages." Its basic nature, however, has been misunderstood. It is, in fact, a prime example of the sacralizing pattern in modern thought.

FICINO

Ficino presents his argument that man is a terrestrial god in Books XIII and XIV of the *Theologia Platonica*. Because he is aware that he is broaching a controversial topic, Ficino takes great care in the earlier books to relate his views to standard themes in philosophy and theology. In Book I, Ficino explains that he intends to resolve a disturbing conflict between theological truths and existential experience. The theological truths are that God created a world in which even the lowest of creatures is able to find happiness and contentment and that man is the highest and most beloved of all the beings God created. The logical conclusion is that man should find greater happiness and satisfaction in the world than do any of God's creatures. But this seems to contradict experience. The beasts seem to find their pleasure in the world more easily than does man.

For Ficino, the resolution of this apparent paradox depends upon a recognition of the distinction between animalic satisfaction and human happiness, and the key is in understanding the uniqueness of the human soul. The soul is a point of intersection between the spiritual and the material, and proper attunement of the soul to the spiritual leads to eternal happiness. A distinctive feature of Ficino's new understanding is its unique integration of the sacred and the secular. Because the sacred is immanent in the secular, there is no disjunction between earthly happiness and heavenly bliss. In fact, it

2. Pico's title for the work was simply *Oratio*. The fuller title was added by enthusiasts who found in it a definitive statement of the Renaissance view of man.

seems that man reaches the pinnacle of his purpose and fulfillment as a terrestrial god and actually loses the principal source of his happiness and dignity when death transports him to Heaven. In Books XIII and XIV, Ficino presents the crucial argument that man's true destiny is to use his God-given powers to rule the created order as a terrestrial god. In Book XIII, Chapter 2, Ficino argues that man's distinction from all other beings is found in his freedom and his independence. Other earthly beings are limited and determined by physical nature and by fate. Man, however, is able to overcome these influences through the highest realms of the intellect.

> [T]he soul is above fate through mind, and in the order of provi-dence only, in such a way that it imitates its superiors and together with them governs inferior beings. For the soul, as though a partici-pant in providence, according to the model of divine governance rules itself, and governs the home, the community, the arts and the ani-mals. . . . Although in these three parts (of ourselves) we are partially bound to the order of things . . . in a fourth we are entirely free and our own. . . .
>
> Sometimes reason adheres to the intellect and then it rises into providence, sometimes it follows the *idolum* [the nether region of the soul, most closely affected by the body] and nature and there it sub-mits to fate by a certain love while trusting the senses it is dis-tracted . . . by the charm of sensible things.[3]

This passage is important because it indicates how Ficino conceives the relation of the physical and the spiritual in the soul and how man is able to draw upon the higher realms to escape determination by the lower. Ficino then explains that the intellectual part supplies the creativity that separates man from other earthly beings. This cre-ative expression ranges from artistic representation, mechanics,

---

3. Even with the renewed attention to Ficino and especially to this text, there is no complete translation of the *Theologia Platonica* in English. The modern critical edition with a French translation is by Raymond Marcel, *Théologie platonicienne de l'immortalité des âmes* (3 vols.; Paris, 1964–70). Quotations cited here are from passages appearing in Charles Trinkaus, *In Our Image and Likeness: Humanity and Divinity in Italian Human-ist Thought* (2 vols.; Chicago, 1970). For comparative purposes, citations will list the Marcel edition and then the Trinkaus translations, which regularly include the origi-nal Latin in the notes. The quotation cited here is a condensation of Marcel, *Théologie*, II, 209ff./Trinkaus, *In Our Image*, II, 477f.

and technology, through which man "imitates all the works of divine nature and perfects, corrects and modifies the works of lower nature," to the highest levels in which man's majesty is demonstrated by his self-governance.[4]

This capacity for self-determination makes man like God and different from all other beings. "The force of man is almost similar to the divine nature since man by himself, that is through his intelligence and skill, governs himself without being in the least limited by his physical nature and imitates the individual works of the higher nature." In elaborating his position, Ficino moves from a description of the elementary levels of self-sufficiency to the highest. Man is "endowed by nature with fewer natural aids to bodily protection than the animals, but he himself provides his own supply of food, clothing, bedding, housing, furnishings and arms." Further, man is capable of creating "an indescribable variety of pleasures . . . for delighting the five senses." More important still, "the cogitative reason . . . [proves] its own inventive genius . . . through various silk and woollen textiles, paintings, sculptures and buildings." The development of the industrial arts is one of man's most significant achievements because it shows "how man everywhere utilises all the materials of the universe as though all were subject to man." Man's real genius, however, is his ability to transform the elements provided by nature to fit his creative purpose. In order to do this, man must possess the same creative capabilities as the divine powers controlling the world: "With celestial virtue he ascends the heavens and measures them. With supercelestial intelligence he transcends the heaven. But man not only uses the elements, he adorns them, which no brute does."[5]

Man's ability to use his "supercelestial intelligence" leads to marvelous accomplishments in the world.

> How stupendous the structures of buildings and cities. How ingenious his works of irrigation. He acts as the vicar of God, since he inhabits all the elements and cultivates all, and present on earth, he is not absent from the ether. Indeed he employs not only the elements

4. Ficino, *Theologia Platonica*, Bk. XIII, Chap. 3; Marcel, II, 223/Trinkaus, II, 482.
5. Marcel, II, 224/Trinkaus, II, 482f.

but all the animals of the elements, terrestrial, aquatic, and flying, for food, comfort and pleasure, and the supernal and celestial ones for learning and the miracles of magic. He not only uses the animals but he rules them. . . . He does not only rule the animals cruelly, but he also governs, fosters and teaches them. *Universal providence is proper to God who is the universal cause. Therefore man who universally provides for all things living and not living is a certain god.* He is the god without doubt of the animals since he uses all of them, rules them, and teaches some of them. He is established also as god of the elements since he inhabits and cultivates them all. He is, finally, the god of all materials since he handles all, and turns and changes them. Anyone who dominates the body in so many and such great things and acts as the vicar of immortal God is without doubt immortal [emphasis added].[6]

This passage constitutes one of the grandest hymns to man's genius in all of Renaissance literature, but Ficino has not yet reached the height of his praise for the god Anthropos. According to Ficino, man is most God-like when he re-creates the heavenly kingdom on earth: "[T]he arts [already described], although they mould the matter of the universe and command the animals, and thus imitate God, the creator of nature, are nevertheless inferior to those arts which imitating the heavenly kingdom undertake the responsibility of human government. . . . [M]an alone so abounds in perfection that he rules himself first, which no beasts do, then governs his family, administers the state, rules peoples and commands the entire world." In these achievements, Ficino says, "[man] is endowed with a genius, as I would put it, that is almost the same as that of the Author of the heavens, and that *man would be able to make the heavens in some way if he only possessed the instruments and the celestial material* [emphasis added]."[7] Further on, Ficino adds that "the mind in comprehending conceives of as many things in itself as God in knowing makes in the world. By speaking it expresses as many into the air; with a reed it writes as many on paper. By making it constructs as many in the material of the world. Therefore he would be proven

6. Trinkaus, II, 483f.
7. Marcel, II, 225–26/Trinkaus, II, 484f.

mad who would deny that the soul, which in the arts and in governing *competes* with God, is divine [emphasis added]."⁸
Man's ability to compete with God extends to working miracles:

> The human mind vindicates to itself a right to divinity not only in
> forming and shaping matter through the methods of arts, as we have
> said, but also in transmuting the species of things by command,
> which work is indeed called a miracle. . . . Here we marvel that the
> souls of men dedicated to God rule the elements, call upon the winds,
> force the clouds to rain, chase away fogs, cure the diseases of human
> bodies and the rest. These plainly were done in certain ages among
> various peoples, as poets sing, historians narrate, and those who are
> the most excellent of philosophers, especially the Platonists, do not
> deny, the ancient theologians testify, above all Hermes and Orpheus,
> and the later theologians also prove by word and deed.⁹

Here is the core of Ficino's "new understanding of human
nature": "The entire striving of our soul is that it become God. Such
striving is no less natural to men than the effort to flight is to
birds."¹⁰ This yearning, which is stronger and more persistent than
any appetite, is placed in us by God. "For who but God, Himself,
whom we seek, would have inserted this into our souls? who, since
He alone is the author of the species, inserts a proper appetite into
the species."¹¹

The next section explains the structure of the soul and the wide
range of human types. It then discusses how man is able to be like
God and how his divinization is accomplished.

> Man leads the life of a plant in so far as in eating he indulges the
> body, the life of an animal when he flatters his senses, the life of a man
> in so far as he consults reason in human affairs, the life of heroes as he

8. Marcel, II, 228–29/Trinkaus, II, 486. The phrase "est aemula Dei," which Trinkaus translated as "competes with God," should perhaps be rendered "strives to equal
God," given the basic meaning of *aemulare*.
9. Ficino, Bk. XIII, Chap. 4; Marcel, II, 229/Trinkaus, II, 486.
10. "Totus igitur animae nostrae conatus est, ut Deus efficatur. Conatus talis
naturalis est hominibus non minus quam conatus avibus ad volandum" (Marcel, II,
247/Trinkaus, II, 487).
11. Marcel, II, 247/Trinkaus, II, 487. Ficino is using a careful rhetorical ploy. Since
the view he is presenting is extremely unorthodox, he attributes it to God's design.

investigates natural phenomena, the life of demons when he engages in mathematical speculation, the life of angels according as he inquires into divine mysteries, the life of God as far as he does all for the sake of God. The soul of every man experiences all these things in a certain way in himself, although each in his own way, and so mankind strives to become all beings since it leads the lives of all beings.[12]

By what instrument and process does man move through the "lives of all beings"? The answer is that the mind in knowing something becomes the thing it knows. Although this epistemological premise may seem strange, it is a basic tenet of Neoplatonic thought. The root of this notion is the Socratic principle that knowledge depends on likeness or similarity between the knower and the known. Anything completely unlike or alien to the knower is incomprehensible. Using this principle, Ficino argues that man knows the world through his participation in it and knows God because of his likeness to Him. This argument, in turn, leads Ficino to conclude that man's discovery of his own ability to know the world and re-create it demonstrates that he shares two of God's primary attributes: comprehensive knowledge and creativity.

Ficino next argues that man's creative involvement in the world is not directed toward physical satisfaction. Instead, his satisfaction is intellectual and spiritual and, in fact, leads to a complete subjugation of the physical. This accomplishment is unique to man—no other being can overcome physical limitations and Fate. Then Ficino makes another exceptional claim: the desire to dominate is not limited to mastery of the physical world. "[T]he immense magnificence of our soul may manifestly be seen from this, that he will not be satisfied with the empire of this world, if, having conquered this one, he learns that there remains another world which he has not yet subjugated. . . . Thus man wishes no superior and no equal and will not permit anything to be left out and excluded from his rule. This status belongs to God alone. Therefore he seeks a divine condition."[13] That is, man will not be satisfied until he is the complete master of his destiny with no dependency on any other being (in-

12. Marcel, II, 252/Trinkaus, II, 489f.
13. Ficino, Bk. XIV, Chap. 4; Marcel, II, 260/Trinkaus, II, 491.

cluding God?). Here we have reached the final stages of Ficino's divinization or sacralization process. The impediments and limitations resulting from man's dualistic nature have been overcome through knowledge. His supercelestial intelligence allows man to control both the secular and the sacred forces influencing the human condition, and through this control man becomes like God.[14]

This "new understanding of human nature" is developed further in the *De vita triplici*. In the introduction, Ficino explains that it is a medical textbook intended for use by scholars to counteract the physical debilitation brought on by their intellectual pursuits. The scope is much broader than this description suggests, however. After presenting medicine as a form of natural magic, Ficino describes magical procedures that are designed to "overcome Fate" and allow man to re-form the world. The *De vita triplici* then moves from discussions of medicine and magic to cosmology. Here Ficino offers a "new understanding" of the world in which the material and the spiritual elements of the cosmos are linked by the world soul (*anima mundi*) and the world spirit (*spiritus mundi*). According to Ficino, the Ancient Wisdom reveals how to draw upon the power of the world spirit to enhance man's physical and spiritual condition and to control the powers of nature in the way the *prisci theologi* did. His discussions of the natural order and man's participation in it has another fundamental purpose as well: to redefine the nature of magic in order to remove apprehensions about its demonic aspects and establish it as the highest form of natural philosophy.

Ficino introduces his work by explaining that he had sought to be a physician of the soul in his previous writings, and now he intends to minister to the general health and well-being of intellectuals, who often neglect the physical in pursuit of the spiritual. In Book I, Ficino explains that scholars are particularly susceptible to melancholia. This condition can be treated, however, by drawing on the beneficial influence of Saturn and other planets favorable to intellectual endeavor. Most of Book I is then given to an account of the substances

14. Ficino's efforts to divinize man pose a fundamental problem that he never addresses. It appears that man is most fully divine while striding the earth as a terrestrial god. Does he not lose his identity and his potency when he is absorbed into immortal union with God?

that contain concentrations of these planetary influences. In the last section, Ficino exhorts scholars to attend to the intellect as well: "It is not all right just to take care of the body, which is only the servant of the soul, and neglect the soul, which is the king and master of the body."[15] The care of the soul, then, becomes the subject of the second book.

Book II acknowledges that a long life is necessary if the scholar is to perfect his knowledge. Long life, however, is not something given by fate. In fact, intellectual efforts have a debilitating effect on the body. There is a solution, however, because man is not like other beings: "Long life is not only a matter of what the Fates have put in store for us from the beginning, but something our diligence takes care of as well."[16]

In Book III, Ficino "explains how man can alter the decrees of fate." The key component is an extended discussion of the interrelation of the material and the spiritual elements in the world. Herein is Ficino's "new understanding" of the world soul and the world spirit. Just as man must have a soul as the mediating link between the material and the spiritual, so must there be a world soul.

> If there were only intellect and body in the world, but no soul, the intellect would not be drawn to the body (for it is altogether immobile, and lacks the affect of motion, as if it were the furthest possible distance from the body), nor would the body be drawn to the intellect, since it is ineffective and inept in itself for such motion, and very remote from the intellect. So if a soul, conforming to each, is placed between them, each one is easily attracted to the other.
> . . . It is connected to all things, in the middle of these things that are distant from each other, for they are not distant from it. It conforms to divine things, and to things fallen, and it verges on each with its affect, and is everywhere all the same.[17]

---

15. Ficino, *Opera Omnia*, I, 559–604. The only complete English translation is *The Book of Life*, trans. Charles Boer (Irving, Tex., 1980). This is a lively, freewheeling translation. Textual citations will note both the original and the translation. Ficino, *De vita*, in *Opera Omnia*, Bk. I, Chap. 31, pp. 538f./Boer (trans.), *Book of Life*, 35.

16. Ficino, Bk. II, Chap. 1, p. 540/Boer, 38.

17. Ficino, Bk. III, Chap. 1, p. 561/Boer, 86f.

In other words, the two opposite parts of the natural world can only be brought together through a mediating link—the world soul. Most important, the world soul includes all the ideal forms in the mind of God. It can thus link them with the material world.

> The soul of the world, the *anima mundi*, divinely contains at least as many seminal reasons for things as there are ideas in the divine mind, and with these reasons it fabricates as many species in matter. Therefore, any species whatsoever answers through its own seminal reasons to its own idea, and can often easily receive through this something from that idea, whenever it is affected through it. Thus, whenever it degenerates from its own form, it can be formed again by this middle thing next to it [*i.e.*, the world soul], and through this middle thing it easily re-forms.[18]

The key passage occurs in the third sentence. Here Ficino indicates that the degeneration and disintegration occurring in "fallen nature" can be overcome by using the world soul to draw the material entity back into conformity with its eternal form or idea. The agent for this re-formation is the world spirit, the force flowing through the world that actually accomplishes the infusion of the divine into the material.

While the world spirit permeates the whole world, it is concentrated in some materials more than others. By using these knowledgeably, man can draw its regenerative benefits into his soul.[19] Ficino contends that the Platonists and the astrologers agree that "[f]rom a certain application of our spirit to the spirit of the world through the art of natural philosophy and through affect, the celestial goods get thrust into our soul and body. This application goes through our spirit, which is in the middle of us, then gets strengthened by the spirit of the world, then through the rays of the stars happily working into our spirit, likewise with rays in nature, and

18. Ficino, Bk. III, Chap. 1, p. 561/Boer, 87.

19. Ficino explains that the fifth essence (*spiritus mundi*) can be absorbed by us, if we know how to separate it from the other elements with which it is heavily mixed, or at least if we know how to use those things that contain it. This is especially true for things in which it is pure, as in select wines and sugars, balsam and gold, precious stones, etc. (Ficino, Bk. III, Chap. 1, 562/Boer, 89).

finally it fits us to the heavens."[20] Ficino then describes the range of
planetary benefits useful to the scholar for maintaining the body
and for cultivating the powers of the mind that can be reached
through the world spirit.[21] Realizing, however, that his move from
conventional medicine to spiritual magic carries him into controversial areas, Ficino prudently notes that his own interest in and use of
these celestial powers are restricted to things within the realm of
natural philosophy and, therefore, consistent with theology.[22]

To underscore that his magic is natural, Ficino explains that it
draws upon the organic interrelation of the material and the spiritual through the world soul and the world spirit.

> Everything we have been talking about comes down to this, that
> our spirit, when it is correctly prepared and cleansed through the
> things of nature, can receive from the spirit of worldly life a great deal
> through the rays of the stars. Since the life of the world is based in
> everything, it is propagated plainly in herbs and trees, as if they were
> hair on its body. It is propagated in stones and metals, as if they were
> its teeth and bones. It is produced in living shells, adhering to rocks
> and earth.
>   . . . [B]y this frequent use of the planets and living things, you will
> be able to draw a great deal from the spirit of the world, especially if
> you do this with living things that are fresh from Mother Earth, as if
> you were being nourished and taken care of by things sticking in
> her.[23]

Ficino begins Chapter 20 by indicating that certain natural substances are so potent with the benefits of the world spirit that,
through them, it is possible to rejuvenate both the body and the soul
so that the recipient seems almost reborn. He adds that astrologers
have contended that the wise man can create images that evoke a
similar power: "They restore him to an even better condition, as if
he had escaped from his old self, or at least they keep one's health
good for long periods of time."[24]

20. Ficino, Bk. III, Chap. 3, p. 564/Boer, 94.
21. These subjects are treated throughout the remainder of Bk. III, but see especially Chaps. 11 and 22.
22. See especially Ficino, Chap. 9, pp. 572ff./Boer, 112ff.
23. Ficino, Bk. III, Chap. 11, pp. 574f./Boer, 115f.
24. Ficino, Bk. III, Chap. 20, pp. 590f./Boer, 155.

Chapter 21 considers the similar magical effects of words, songs, and music. Chapter 22 contains a restatement of the sympathetic links between the natural world and the celestial and supercelestial powers. One passage provides an excellent summary and will be quoted at length.

> Because heaven has been composed by a harmonic cause, and because it is moved harmonically, and affects everything with harmonic movements and sounds, it is right that through this harmony alone not only men but all lower things are prepared to take the heavenly gifts for their powers. We divide up this vast harmony of higher things into seven grades of things: images that are harmonically constituted, medicines tempered with a certain consonance, vapors and odors that are made with a similar concinnity, and musical songs and sounds.
>
> We want to add to this list the force got out of gestures of the body, dancing, and ritual movement, through concepts of the imagination, harmonious movements, agreeable discourses of reason, and tranquil contemplations of the mind. For just as we expose the body through its daily harmony (that is, through its habits and customs), and its image, to the light and heat of the Sun, we also acquire the spirit that is hidden in the powers of the stars through a similar kind of harmony. . . .
>
> Then, finally, through the spirit that is thus prepared in the planets (as we have often said) we expose the soul and the body to them. We expose the soul, I say, to the extent that it is inclined to the spirit and body through affect. . . .
>
> Likewise our reason . . . can, by a kind of imitation, put itself in agreement with Jove. . . .
>
> Finally, the contemplative mind, to the extent that it calls itself away not only from those things which we feel but even from those which we imagine and which we prove in human affairs, calls itself away in affect, intention, and in life, and calls itself back to separate things—to this extent it exposes itself to Saturn.[25]

Ficino then refers to the Ancient Wisdom to support his claim for the benefits of attunement to planetary influences, particularly Saturn and the Moon. First of all, these texts affirm the physical benefits: "This is why those Lunar people whom Socrates describes in the

25. Ficino, Bk. III, Chap. 22, pp. 594ff./Boer, 164f.

Phaedo, living on the highest surface of the earth, higher than the clouds, seeing things soberly and content with only fruits to eat, with the zeal of a secret wisdom and a religion devoted to Saturn, enjoyed happiness. They lived such a prosperous and long life that they were said not to be mortal men at all but immortal daemons, whom many heroes celebrate, a golden race enjoying Saturn's time and reign." Farther on, Ficino describes the planetary scheme most beneficial to the philosopher-magus in his intellectual pursuits: "By this arrangement, the Chaldeans and Egyptians and the Platonists thought one could avoid the malignity of fate. . . . [I]t is no wonder that they not only wanted to obtain the many things that pertain to man's body and spirit there, but the many good things as well that overflow for the soul, not from bodies into the soul, but from souls. Many more things of this kind, however, flow forth from the higher minds in heaven." Through such a concerted use of the natural influences resident in the material world and through the evocation of celestial powers through spiritual magic, "we break away from fate."[26]

Ficino then provides a further explanation of magic as basic to science and technology.

> If we turn to agriculture, one prepares a field and seeds for heavenly gifts, and with certain graftings one propagates the life of a plant, leading to another and a better species. Doctors, physicians, and surgeons do similar things in our own bodies to nourish them and to make them acquire more richly the nature of the universe. A philosopher learned in natural and astral matters, whom we call therefore a Magus, does the same thing, with certain earthly enticements drawing the heavenly things when he does it properly, sowing no differently than a farmer who is knowledgeable in grafting, who starts a new shoot off old stock.

Ficino again supports his position by invoking ancient authority. "This is exactly what Ptolemy said, too, agreeing that a man who is wise in this way can help in the work of the stars just like a farmer can in working the power of the earth. A magus subjects earthly things to the heavens, the lower to the higher, so that everywhere

26. Ficino, Bk. III, Chap. 22, p. 595/Boer, 166f.

things that are feminine are made fertile by things that are masculine, as iron is drawn to a magnet."[27] The magus' creative powers are, then, like the farmer's. Both are capable of improving existing species and creating new ones.

This passage is followed by a discussion of controversial accounts of the *prisci theologi* drawing celestial powers into statues, a feat attributed to unorthodox demonic magic. Ficino defends the *prisci theologi*, however, by maintaining that the same could be accomplished through acceptable spiritual magic with the world soul as the agent.

> But let us get back to Mercurius—in fact, let us get back to Plotinus! Mercurius said priests received a power that was from the nature of the world, and that this was mixed. Plotinus, following him, thinks that everything can be easily conciliated in the soul of the world to the extent that it generates and moves the forms of natural things through certain seminal reasons divinely inside it. He even calls these reasons Gods, because they are never apart from the ideas of the supreme mind.
>
> Therefore, through reasons of this kind, the soul of the world easily applies itself to materials which it formed from the very beginning through these. Some magus or priest will then use the forms of these things, collecting them correctly and at the right times.[28]

Toward the end of this work, Ficino again describes medicine and all other forms of improvement of life as *natural* magic—whether it be the work of the physician, the farmer, or the magician. "Nature," says Ficino, "is everywhere a magician."[29] This argument is developed slowly and cautiously. He first explains that accepted medical techniques involving diet and other regulatory practices derive their effectiveness from the stars (a standard belief in his day). This is possible, according to Ficino, because the world spirit links the divine ideas with the world substance. Medicine, properly understood, therefore, is the practical knowledge of planetary influences resident in natural substances. Having established this fundamental notion, Ficino broadens his application to prolonging life and to

27. Ficino, Bk. III, Chap. 26, p. 600/Boer, 179f.
28. Ficino, Bk. III, Chap. 26, p. 601/Boer, 182.
29. Ficino, Bk. III, Chap. 26, p. 600/Boer, 179.

ministering to the soul and the mind. These measures are possible because the *spiritus* is resident in the soul and is able through it to affect the intelligence.

This extended discussion of medicine's relation to magic is crucial to Ficino's defense of the wider application of magic. His primary aim is to establish an analogy between the physician's knowledge of the well-being of the body and the magus' knowledge of the needs of the soul and intellect. Moreover, Ficino intends to move his magic away from the proscriptions against trafficking with demons: his magic draws upon the *spiritus mundi* and is, therefore, *natural* and acceptable to the Church. Ficino reinforces this claim by developing the analogy between the farmer and the magus. Both draw upon natural forces to improve and to change the physical world for the benefit of man.

The important point is that Ficino's reformulation of magic provides the epistemological foundation for a new image of man as the master of the natural world and the shaper of his own destiny. This is essential to Ficino's description of man as a terrestrial god. Furthermore, a fundamental reconceptualization of God and the world is integral to the development of Ficino's new understanding of human nature. This reconceptualization is oriented around the root concept of the world soul that links the material world to the ideal forms that give it its beauty and its purpose. The most important element of Ficino's discussion of the world soul for our consideration is his claim that any degeneration or disorder in the natural world can be corrected by reinfusing the material world with supercelestial influences. Because man's own soul is a microcosm of this macrocosmic order, he can participate directly in the restoration of order and in the creation of beauty and harmony. We have in this notion, then, a full presentation of the concept of sacralization. The sacred is the source of order, beauty, and harmony in the secular world; the secular is the incarnation of the divine. This world is created by God and intended to be man's home. Moreover, man is able to obtain the knowledge and the creative power to create beauty and harmony in the world and to shape his own destiny. It is this ability that justifies Ficino's description of man as a terrestrial god in the *Theologia Platonica*.

Pico

It is well known that the purpose of the *Oration on Human Dignity* was to provide a concise statement of Pico's understanding of human nature and of knowledge, which he expanded upon in the nine hundred propositions he offered to debate with the doctors of the Church. Pico begins the *Oration* by indicating that he intends to develop a new perspective on the nature of man and his place in God's creation. His point of departure is the affirmation by Hermes Trismegistus and other *prisci theologi* that man is the greatest miracle of creation. The difficulty is that conventional views of man do not explain why or how he can be the *magnum miraculum*. In fact, other beings—angels and star demons, for example—appear to hold a far loftier position than does man. In order to set the record straight, Pico offers a new myth of creation. "God the Father, the supreme Architect, had already built this cosmic home we behold, the most sacred temple of His godhead, by the laws of His mysterious wisdom. The region above the heavens He had adorned with Intelligences, the heavenly spheres He had quickened with eternal souls, and the excrementary and filthy parts of the lower world He had filled with a multitude of animals of every kind." Having finished his creation, God longed to have "someone to ponder the plan of so great a work, to love its beauty, and to wonder at its vastness." He therefore decided to create man: "He finally took thought concerning the creation of man. But there was not among His archetypes that from which He could fashion a new offspring, nor was there in His treasure-houses anything which He might bestow on His new son as an inheritance, nor was there in the seats of all the world a place where the latter might sit to contemplate the universe. All was now complete; all things had been assigned to the highest, the middle, and the lowest orders."[30]

Because man could not be given special or unique features, God gave him a composite nature with unlimited potential to be whatever he decides. "He therefore took man as a creature of indeterminate nature and, assigning him a place in the middle of the world,

30. Quotations are from the Elizabeth Forbes translation, which appears in Ernst Cassirer, P. O. Kristeller, and J. H. Randall, Jr. (eds.), *The Renaissance Philosophy of Man* (Chicago, 1948). The citations are found on p. 224.

addressed him thus: 'Neither a fixed abode nor a form that is thine alone nor any function peculiar to thyself have we given thee, Adam, to the end that according to thy longing and according to thy judgment thou mayest have and possess what abode, what form, and what functions thou thyself shalt desire.' " All other beings, even the celestial demons, have a fixed nature.

> Thou, constrained by no limits, in accordance with thine own free will, in whose hand We have placed thee, shalt ordain for thyself the limits of thy nature. We have set thee at the world's center that thou mayest from thence more easily observe whatever is in the world. We have made thee neither of heaven nor of earth, neither mortal nor immortal, so that with freedom of choice and with honor, as though the maker and molder of thyself, thou mayest fashion thyself in whatever shape thou shalt prefer. . . .
>
> If sensitive, he will become brutish. If rational, he will grow into a heavenly being. If intellectual, he will be an angel and the son of God. And if, happy in the lot of no created thing, he withdraws into the center of his own unity, his spirit, made one with God, in the solitary darkness of God, who is set above all things, shall surpass them all.[31]

Pico implores his fellow man to use his full potential: "Let a certain holy ambition invade our souls, so that, not content with the mediocre, we shall pant after the highest and (since we may if we wish) toil with all our strength to obtain it. . . . Let us disdain earthly things, despise heavenly things, and, finally, esteeming less whatever is of the world, hasten to that court which is beyond the world and nearest to the Godhead." But how do we go about our divinization? Pico's answer is, at least at first appearance, a conventional one: "Let us go to the ancient fathers who, inasmuch as they were familiar and conversant with these matters, can give sure and altogether trustworthy testimony."[32]

According to the ancient masters, the first step in the process is "washing away the filth of ignorance and vice, cleanse our soul, so that her passions may not rave at random nor her reason through heedlessness ever be deranged." This process of purification is the path of natural philosophy. When we take that path, we will turn

---

31. Cassirer, Kristeller, and Randall (eds.), *Renaissance Philosophy,* 224f.
32. *Ibid.,* 227f.

from superficial and meaningless affairs toward the eternal. But, as Pico adds, "it is not, therefore, in the power of natural philosophy to give us in nature a true quiet and unshaken peace but that this is the function and privilege of her mistress, that is, of holiest theology." The theology that Pico refers to is the collected wisdom of the *prisci theologi*. Provided to man directly by God, the ancient theology has been preserved in writings that are deliberately confusing to the ignorant but clear to the wise. For those capable of understanding these teachings, the path to divinization is sure and certain. Again, Pico appeals not only to the Judaeo-Christian mystical teachings but to the full range of ancient theology to verify his contention that following this path of knowledge entitles mankind to "become He Himself Who made us."[33]

Having established the path to be taken from natural philosophy through the occult teachings of the ancient theologians, Pico describes his own knowledge system and its contribution. First, Pico claims the notable achievement of having assembled an extraordinary library of documents of the Ancient Wisdom. This recovery of these precious documents will in itself serve as a means of overcoming the ignorance and error that have afflicted human philosophizing and theologizing. But Pico says that his achievement is not simply as collector. His distinctive accomplishment is that he has drawn together and reconciled the essential core of these various teachings into a single coherent system "by means of which whoever holds them will be able . . . to answer any question whatever proposed in natural philosophy or divinity."[34]

After briefly discussing his reconciliation of Platonic and Aristotelian thought and his integration of the various other traditions into a coherent philosophy, Pico states that he has also established the proper role of magic in philosophy and theology. In this segment he is quick to say that demonic magic is to be avoided, but that natural magic, "when it is rightly pursued, is nothing else than the utter perfection of natural philosophy." To defend this controversial view, Pico cites the Ancient Wisdom and the many *prisci theologi* who

---

33. *Ibid.*, 229, 231, 234. Pico adds that his system is "other than we are taught in that philosophy which is studied in the schools and practiced by doctors of this age."
34. Cassirer, Kristeller, and Randall (eds.), *Renaissance Philosophy*, 245.

regard magic as "a perfect and most high wisdom." Pico then examines the nature of the magic that these ancient traditions hold in such high esteem: "If we ask Plato what the magic of both these men was, he will reply, in his *Alcibiades*, that the magic of Zoroaster was none other than the science of the Divine in which the kings of the Persians instructed their sons, to the end that they might be taught to rule their own commonwealth by the example of the commonwealth of the world. He will answer, in the *Charmides*, that the magic of Zamolxis was that medicine of the soul through which temperance is brought to the soul as through temperance health is brought to the body."[35] The two magical traditions that Plato cites have had many noble followers. Pico suggests that the number of magi is even larger than has been recognized thus far and that he will prove this in his forthcoming *Poetic Theology.*[36]

Having identified magic as the highest form of philosophizing and linked it to the Ancient Wisdom, Pico turns to the question of how magic operates. He is again broaching controversial areas, but does so in a way that is intended to obscure the unorthodox nature of his position. In this discussion, Pico is careful to indicate that the magicians use natural rather than demonic magic. His description of natural magic, however, extends much farther than is usually permitted. The magician calls "into the light as if from their hiding-places the powers scattered and sown in the world by the loving Kindness of God." Being able to perform magic rests upon "having more searchingly examined into the harmony of the universe, . . . and having clearly perceived the reciprocal affinity of natures, and applying to each single thing the suitable and peculiar inducements . . . [to bring] into the open the miracles concealed in the recesses of the world, in the depths of nature, and in the storehouses and mysteries of God." To underscore that this magic is natural, Pico introduces an analogy much like Ficino's in the *De vita:* "As the farmer weds his elms to vines, even so does the *magus* wed earth to heaven, that is, he weds lower things to the endowments and powers of higher things." The magician's endeavors finally have as their purpose the arousal of love and admiration for God

35. *Ibid.*, 247f.
36. This work was never completed.

and His creation: "For nothing moves one to religion and to the worship of God more than the diligent contemplation of the wonders of God; if we have thoroughly examined them by this natural magic we are considering, we shall be compelled to sing, more ardently inspired to the worship and love of the Creator: 'The heavens and all the earth are full of the majesty of thy glory.' And [Pico concludes] this is enough about magic."[37]

If we compare this characterization with Pico's creation myth, we begin to understand how central magic is to the fulfillment of human destiny. According to his myth, God created man so there would exist a being who could "ponder the plan of so great a work, to love its beauty, and to wonder at its vastness." The purpose of magic is the "diligent contemplation of the wonders of God [that] inspire[s] . . . worship and love of the Creator." Therefore, it seems that the being created to know and to appreciate His universe is the magician. It is also the magician, and only the magician, who can attain self-divinization and employ his knowledge to order and perfect society.

It is evident that Pico's myth is indebted to the creation account found in the *Corpus Hermeticum*. In the *Pimander* or *Poimandres*, Hermes Trismegistus has revealed to him the true nature of the world and of man. The Demiurge created the world, but the divine Father created man. So man is beautiful and shares in the divine power. As primal man looks down on the universe, he expresses his wish to use his divinely given creative powers and obtains permission from God to assist the Demiurge in creation of the natural order. Primal man is taught the essence of the workings of the universe, and he is thus able to become a creator as well. Pico has modified this story, eliminating the Demiurge and having God perform both acts of creation, but the essence of the story remains. Man is a special creation of God with divine powers. When Pico's full narrative in the *Oration* is taken into account, there is a strong suggestion that the magus is the reincarnation of primal man. He has the power to create in the physical world because he has been empowered by God and because the lesser orders of being that control the operations of the natural world taught him nature's secrets.

37. Cassirer, Kristeller, and Randall (eds.), *Renaissance Philosophy*, 248f.

While Pico's myth closely parallels the Hermetic view, its concept of man contrasts sharply with the Judaeo-Christian creation stories. In Pico's myth, man has no boundaries to his nature; he can be whatever he wills to be. Also, man's desire for God-like knowledge serves as a bond between man and God, not as a source of sin and alienation.

In the next chapter we will examine the influence of Ficino's and Pico's new understanding of human nature in two areas of sixteenth- and seventeenth-century thought: the mounting criticism of traditional theology and metaphysics as forms of ignorance and alienation, and the rise of utopian dreams of innerworldly perfection. Before we turn to this next stage of analysis, however, it is important to once again draw the lines of contrast between the pattern of sacralization and secularization.

Sacralization	*Secularization*
Man: a terrestrial god, master of nature and destiny	Man: subject to Fate and Necessity
God: immanent, created man to be co-creator	God: remote or completely absent from the world
Nature: divine creation, malleable, perfectible by man	Nature: closed system, indifferent to man
Society: microcosm of macrocosmic harmony, realm of man's greatest creativity	Society: controlled by Fate, Necessity, human appetite and need

Although the two conceptions are virtually diametrically opposed, they are nevertheless complementary. They contribute to the breakdown of traditional Judaeo-Christian dualism and create the epochal consciousness that separates modernity from the medieval period.

Chapter Four

SACRALIZATION IN THE SIXTEENTH AND SEVENTEENTH CENTURIES

In the sixteenth and seventeenth centuries the sacralizing emphasis shifts from projects of self-divinization to utopian dreams of religious and political reformation. This shift is readily apparent in the writings of three major writers of the time: Cornelius Agrippa, Giordano Bruno, and Tommaso Campanella. Agrippa attacks Church corruption and theological confusion as evidence of a profound state of alienation and disorder. Like the Protestant reformers, Agrippa calls for a recovery of pristine Christianity, but his is an esoteric Christianity closely tied to the Cabala. Bruno also criticizes the intellectual and spiritual disorientation of the Church and calls for a re-institution of Hermetic religion as a replacement for Christianity. Campanella, the author of the famous utopia, *La Città del Sole,* leads a revolt that is intended to establish a Hermetic City of the Sun as the new political and religious center of Western civilization. Through an examination of their writings, it is possible to see how the sacralizing tradition serves as a source for the modern vision of an epochal break with the Christian "dark age" and for the advent of modern messianic figures who propose to lead man out of his alienated condition into a utopian paradise.

AGRIPPA

Charles Nauert, who is the principal contemporary interpreter of Agrippa, has called him an extraordinary man in an age of extraordinary men.[1] Agrippa himself claimed to know seven languages and to have mastered the liberal arts, theology, and law. While there is, obviously, a good deal of self-promotion in his claims, it is nevertheless true that Agrippa's command of languages and his extensive acquaintance with ancient texts gained him an international reputation as an authority on ancient learning. Moreover, his critical writings on theology and philosophy attracted the interest of both Protestant and Catholic reformers.[2] Modern scholars, on the other hand, have held mixed opinions about Agrippa's role in the sixteenth century. Those who have concentrated on his famous *De Occulta Philosophia* have considered him a propagator of superstition and pseudo-science at odds with the modern currents in sixteenth-century thought.[3] By contrast, scholars who have given primary weight to his later *De Incertitudine et Vanitate Scientiarum et Artium* have found in this text a brilliant criticism of the intellectual confusion of scholastic philosophy and theology and a perceptive attack on esoteric knowledge and pseudo-science.[4] From this perspective, then, Agrippa emerges as one of the forerunners of modern skepticism and early positivism.

When Agrippa's epistemological perspective is properly understood, however, there is no fundamental change in his position from the early writings to the last. Throughout his scholarly efforts, he was convinced that the present state of learning reflected a sense of disorientation and confusion that had to be overcome for man to regain his full humanity. It is this conviction that prompts his criticisms both of traditional theology and philosophy and certain dimensions of the Ancient Wisdom that he felt had become corrupted and disoriented.

1. Charles G. Nauert, Jr., *Agrippa and the Crisis of Renaissance Thought* (Urbana, Ill., 1965).

2. His rigorous attacks on traditional thought also led to aggressive counterattacks by university professors and the doctors of the Church. The faculty of the Sorbonne, for example, condemned his *De vanitate*.

3. This work was written in 1509–10 and circulated in manuscript. It was not published until 1531–32. Despite Agrippa's importance and the current interest in him, critical editions of his major works are still unavailable. For a listing of commonly used editions, see the bibliography in Nauert, *Agrippa and the Crisis*, 336f.

4. *De vanitate* was prepared in the summer of 1526 and first published in 1530. An English translation appeared in 1569. See Nauert, *Agrippa and the Crisis*, 337.

The key to understanding the continuity in Agrippa's major writings is in his abiding interest in laying the foundations for a recovery of the essential core of God's revelation to man and thereby overcoming man's fundamental alienation from his role as a terrestrial god. A useful text for understanding Agrippa's position is an early work entitled *De Triplici Ratione cognoscendi Deum* (1516). In this book Agrippa cites the widespread corruption and spiritual disorder in the Church as evidence that Christianity has lost its anchoring in the primary revelations of God. Agrippa identifies two principal sources for this state of alienation and confusion. His primary criticism is directed toward the scholastic effort to make theology commensurable with classical philosophy. For Agrippa, this enterprise shows a failure to recognize the distinction between the knowledge provided through direct revelation by God and the informed opinions derived from man's sensory experience and deductive reasoning. Agrippa is also highly critical of the revival of the Latin humanist tradition, which also places undue emphasis on human reason and imagination.

To explain the cause of this intellectual disorientation, Agrippa provides an interpretation that links the disorder of the current age to the intellectual and spiritual alienation resulting from Adam's sin. While this is a standard theme, Agrippa gives it a novel twist. Agrippa does not attribute Adam's sin to his effort to obtain God-like knowledge. Instead, Adam sins by indulging his animalic senses and the lower forms of reason rather than using his God-like knowledge to become creatively involved in shaping the world. This intriguing interpretation is also important to understanding Agrippa's prescription for overcoming intellectual disorientation.

As the title *De Triplici Ratione* suggests, Agrippa finds three paths provided by God to enable man to overcome his ignorance and alienation and recover his full humanity: the book of nature, the book of law, and the gospel. At first glance, this description seems similar to traditional scholasticism. But as Agrippa proceeds it becomes clear that his position is quite different. For Agrippa, the key to a proper understanding of nature, the law, and the gospel is the teaching of the *prisci theologi*. Like Ficino, Agrippa is convinced that the ancient theologies have a core that can serve as the means of recovering the essence of Christianity. There is one significant difference, however. For Ficino, the primary guide to understanding the Ancient Wisdom was Hermes Trismegistus, who was regarded as the teacher of both Plato and Moses. For Agrippa, the primary source is not the Hermetic teachings but the Cabala, the Jewish esoteric tradition supposedly given to Moses during his forty days and nights on Mount Sinai. According to this view, the law expressed in the Decalogue is only a minor part of God's revelation. The deeper part was not made public; it was kept among a highly select group of priests who were able to understand its full import. In Agrippa's time a Christianized Cabala was emerging. This stressed the magical elements of the Cabalist tradition as the true core of Judaism, which could be directly linked with the essence of Christianity revealed in the teachings and miracles of the Messiah.[5]

In describing the three paths open to man, Agrippa places the conventional approaches in juxtaposition to the true understanding revealed in the ancient teachings. In its broadest application, this is a contrast between the intellectual disorder resulting from Adam's squandering the highest forms of esoteric knowledge and the magus' using that knowledge to become a terrestrial god. From this perspective, nature—the first of Agrippa's three paths to true knowledge—can only be understood properly if one follows the occult teachings of the Ancient Wisdom. On this point, Agrippa's position is similar to Ficino's effort to develop a cosmology that links the physical and the spiritual worlds and connects man's knowledge of the cosmos with the power to restore nature and to perfect the human condition. His perspective on the law, the second path, derives from the Cabalist tradition, which he is convinced provides the power to ascend through the orders of nature to direct communion with God. Thus man gains full knowledge of the workings of nature and the operative power to change the con-

5. Pico was a principal contributor to the development of a Christianized Cabala. See Frances Yates, *The Occult Philosophy in the Elizabethan Age* (London, 1979), especially Chap. 2; for a discussion of Agrippa's Cabala, see Yates, *Occult Philosophy*, Chaps. 5 and 6. For a general discussion of the development of the Christianized Cabala, see J. L. Blau, *The Christian Interpretation of the Cabala in the Renaissance* (Port Washington, N.Y., 1944); and François Secret, *Les Kabbalistes chrétiens de la Renaissance* (Paris, 1964).

ditions of existence. The return to the gospel, the third path, is through a reading of the Ancient Wisdom traditions, finally clarifying the role God wants man to assume.

This brief discussion demonstrates that Agrippa continues the efforts of Ficino and Pico to establish the unifying core of the revelations given by God and to use it to recover the full understanding of man's nature. If we now briefly reconsider Agrippa's linking man's alienation to the sin of Adam, we see a novel integration of the Christian myth of Adam's fall with the Hermetic myths of man's creation by God. For Agrippa, man's true condition is the one described in the "Egyptian Genesis." God created man to be a terrestrial god. For reasons that are never clear, however, man becomes disoriented and alienated from his true nature. To guide man back, God has provided the *prisca theologia*. Again, for unexplained reasons, man lost the ability to understand and use it. Now, however, recovering the hidden truth of the Ancient Wisdom allows Agrippa and other wise men to gain a comprehensive understanding of these revelations and thereby recognize the source of man's alienation and overcome it. It is with this conviction that Agrippa undertakes his famous text, *De Occulta Philosophia*.

The *De Occulta* is an account of the principles and procedures of magical operations based on the Ancient Wisdom tradition. In preparing this text, Agrippa is comparable to a Renaissance humanist. He draws upon his considerable skill with languages and his familiarity with a wide range of texts to establish what he considers the earliest and most reliable texts. He then attempts to eliminate errors and inaccuracies that accumulated in later texts and traditions of interpretation. His ultimate purpose is to use these texts to establish the foundation for the recovery of man's knowledge of the world and thereby to restore his role as a terrestrial god. It is not necessary to examine this text in detail here.[6] The essential purpose was established through the discussion of the *De Triplici Ratione*. Moreover, the *De Occulta* is, for the most part, a manual of operations and not a theoretical text. Its three principal divisions set forth the basic pro-

6. For discussions reflecting current scholarship, see Nauert, *Agrippa and the Crisis;* Yates, *Occult Philosophy;* and Shumaker, *Occult Sciences in the Renaissance.*

cedures for magical operations that proceed from the terrestrial to the celestial and finally to the supercelestial realm. The theories behind these operations resemble closely those we examined in Ficino's *Theologia Platonica* and *De vita triplici*. Like Ficino, Agrippa identifies the source of man's capacity for performing magic as the correspondence between the structure of the human soul and the structure of the world soul. There is, again, one basic difference. Ficino gave primacy to the Hermetic materials in developing his concept of natural magic; Agrippa is convinced that God's fullest revelation outside Christianity occurs in the Cabala.

The *De Occulta* was one of the most widely known texts in the sixteenth century and contributed to Agrippa's growing international reputation as the master magician of his age. This reputation gained him invitations as a university lecturer and as a counselor to royal courts. Given his renown as "one of the most extraordinary men of an extraordinary age," it is puzzling that some twenty years after preparing the *De Occulta*, he published the *De vanitate*, a scathing attack on the vanity and futility of all forms of human knowledge.[7] In this work, Agrippa uses his command of philosophy, theology, the humanist tradition, and the occult tradition to argue that all these modes of inquiry have been corrupted through sin and have led to human suffering and alienation from God. Some critics regard this attack as a bold statement of Agrippa's disenchantment with the various metaphysical systems of his age and often consider it one of the early prototypes of the skepticism that emerged in the seventeenth century. Other scholars, however, question the sincerity of Agrippa's position in the *De vanitate*, arguing that the Church's changing attitude toward magic during the Counter-Reformation made him prudently bring his position into closer alignment with orthodox views. But Agrippa's basic point of view in the *De vanitate* is not a departure from the position in the *De Triplici Ratione* or the *De Occulta*.

The *De vanitate* criticizes conventional philosophy and theology, the revival of humanism, and the distortion and corruption of God's revelation in the Ancient Wisdom. Little needs to be said about

---

7. As already noted, *De Occulta* (1509–10) was not published until 1531–32, when attitudes toward magic were changing.

Agrippa's criticisms of the first two categories, since his stance is consistent with that in the *De Triplici Ratione*. The criticisms of the occult wisdom, however, do need explanation in light of the *De Occulta*. A closer examination of his criticisms of the Ancient Wisdom show that they are directed at two elements. The first is astrology and other divinatory systems. In fact, Agrippa, like Ficino and Pico, rejects astrology because its basic premise is that man's fate is knowable because it is determined by the stars. Agrippa maintains that man can use astral magic to manipulate the stars and other celestial divinities to serve his own purpose and to alter his fate.

Agrippa also criticizes the occult wisdom on the basis of the Hermetic materials and the Cabala. Here he does seem to be making a significant departure, but closer examination shows that this is not the case. In Agrippa's view, the Hermetic materials were important, but they were not the primary source of ancient learning. Therefore, when he claims in the *De vanitate* that these materials in themselves are not a sufficient guide to knowledge and that if used by themselves they lead to sin, he is not significantly altering his opinion. His attack on the Cabala also turns out to be consistent with his earlier position. In the Jewish Cabala, he criticizes particularly those elements that develop after the coming of Christ and show a deliberate disregard for the higher truth revealed by the Messiah. He continues, however, to value those elements of the Cabala that point toward the fuller Christian revelation. This position is consistent with that taken in both the *De Triplici Ratione* and the *De Occulta*. Throughout his life, Agrippa was convinced that the key to recovering man's true nature was in a proper reading and understanding of the Christian revelation. Furthermore, the key to this revelation was not in the literal words of the gospel but in their secret, esoteric meaning that could be brought to light by use of the Cabala and other Ancient Wisdom traditions.

It is also important to note that Agrippa's views of the source of knowledge and the concept of man are not altered in the *De vanitate*. Magic is not included in the sciences that he criticizes. In fact, it is the "highest peak of natural philosophy." This magic is the key to restoring man as a terrestrial god and the means for overcoming the alienated state produced by Adam's sin. Further evidence that Agrippa's position remained basically unchanged in his later years is in an important letter that Nauert has called attention to. In this letter written two years after the *De vanitate,* Agrippa acknowledges that there are "natural sciences, metaphysical arts, and occult devices . . . whereby one can licitly defend kingdoms, increase wealth, and cure sickness."[8] This description is consistent with Agrippa's earliest position. He drew upon the emphasis in the sacralizing tradition on the recovery of knowledge that enables man to transform the conditions of his existence and to perfect society.

If we now briefly review Agrippa's fundamental concerns, it becomes clear that they are comparable to those of the religious reformers and of the "secularizers" of the period. Agrippa's response, however, is substantially different and shows the distinctive features of the sacralizing tradition in contrast to both orthodox thought and secular views. His attacks on the corruption of the Church and the ignorance and error of scholastic philosophy and humanism are similar to those of Luther, for example. What is more, both see the solution to the present disorder in a return to a pure form of gospel Christianity. Their understanding of what constitutes this pristine course, however, is very different. For Luther, it is realigning the teachings and practices of the Church with primitive Christianity; for Agrippa, it is recovering the hidden wisdom of the gospel revelations. Luther and Agrippa also hold fundamentally different views of man's proper relation to God. Luther sees a gulf separating sinful man from his righteous God, and only divine action can bridge it. While Agrippa agrees with Luther's description of the human condition after Adam's sin, he is convinced that this unnatural state can be overcome through a recovery of the ancient knowledge. When man makes the effort to reorient his soul and recover his true nature, he will be restored as a terrestrial god capable of finding his purpose and fulfillment through his action in the world. The basic contrast between the two is most concisely expressed in their respective views of Adam's sin. For Luther, it is man's desire to gain knowledge to be like God. For Agrippa, it is in

8. Nauert, *Agrippa and the Crisis,* 216.

man's choosing a sentient life in which he worships the creation rather than the Creator and thereby disregards the higher forms of knowledge that can put him in direct communion with God and enable him to be an active participant in the creation.

There are basic differences between Agrippa's position and the secularizing tradition as well. Agrippa shares with Machiavelli the cynical assessment of the current state of human existence. Society is governed by the selfish, animalic interests of the citizenry and by the desire for self-aggrandizement of political leaders. Machiavelli believes that recognizing this essential condition is the beginning of a realistic concept of human nature and of politics. For Agrippa, the present state of affairs is the result of a profound intellectual and spiritual disorientation that can be corrected through the restoration of the Ancient Wisdom, which can in turn bring about the perfection of man and of society.

The point of comparison with Galileo is their shared criticism of medieval natural philosophy. Like Galileo, Agrippa believes that the prevailing world picture is the result of epistemological errors that distort the natural order; and, like Galileo, Agrippa attempts to open new perspectives on the laws of nature. Agrippa would, however, regard Galileo's inductive, empirical approach as unreliable because it depends too heavily on man's flawed senses and the errors of human observation and analysis. For Agrippa, the path to the understanding of nature is in the teachings and in the magical operations set out in the Ancient Wisdom.

BRUNO

There is a long-standing view of Bruno as a martyr to the cause of modern science. Thanks primarily to the work of Frances Yates, it is now clear that Bruno's interest in and commitment to the defense of the Copernican system had a source very different from Galileo's. For Bruno, the Copernican system represented a recovery of the Ancient Wisdom's view of the universe and signaled the beginning of a general recovery of the ancient tradition, which would produce a thoroughgoing religious and political reformation. This brief examination focuses on Bruno's vision of the beginning of a new age and on his messianic role.[9] One of his early writings, *La Cena de le ceneri* (1584), is his account of a dinner at Oxford in which he defended the Copernican view against the "pedantry" of the university's philosophers and theologians. It may initially seem to be similar to Galileo's famous *Dialogo dei due massimi sistemi del mondo* (1632), in which the Copernican theory is defended against philosophical and theological criticisms. Closer examination of Bruno's work makes clear, however, that the two are markedly different. In his dialogue Bruno criticizes the general state of learned ignorance among university philosophers and Church theologians in ways that recall Agrippa's criticisms in the *De Triplici Ratione* and the *De vanitate*. Also, like Agrippa, Bruno maintains that the way out of that state is through the teachings of the "Chaldeans, of the Egyptians, of the Magi, of the Orphics, of the Pythagoreans and other early thinkers."[10] Bruno reveres Copernicus' work because he thinks it is inspired by this Ancient Wisdom tradition and therefore signals a recovery of the true understanding of the cosmos. "Who then would treat this man (Copernicus) and his labours with such ignoble discourtesy as to forget all his achievements and his divinely ordained appearance as the dawn which was to precede the full sunrise of the ancient and true philosophy after its agelong burial in the dark caverns of blind and envious ignorance." From subsequent passages, it becomes clear that Bruno regards the Copernican theory as a first step in a wholesale recovery of the Ancient Wisdom and that Bruno will lead the way. Bruno's description of his own achievement in relation to that of Copernicus suggests that he saw the latter as a sort of John the Baptist who paves the way for his messianic role.

> What then shall be said of him who has found a way to mount up to the sky . . . ? The Nolan . . . has released the human spirit, and set knowledge at liberty. Man's mind was suffocating in the close air of a

9. This discussion follows closely Frances Yates's analysis in *Giordano Bruno*, 190–359.

10. Yates, *Giordano Bruno*, 235. The original Italian text is found in Giordano Bruno, *Dialoghi italiani*, ed. G. Gentile (Firenze, 1957), 41. Citations will note both the original and the translation.

narrow prison house whence only dimly, and, as it were, through chinks could he behold the far distant stars. His wings were clipped, so that he might not soar upwards through the cloudy veil to see what really lies beyond it and liberate himself from the foolish imaginations of those who—issuing from the miry caverns of earth as though they were Mercuries and Apollos descending from heaven—have with many kinds of deceit imposed brutal follies and vices upon the world in the guise of virtues, of divinity and discipline, quenching the light which rendered the souls of our fathers in antique times divine and heroic whilst confirming and approving the pitch dark ignorance of fools and sophists. . . . Behold now, standing before you, the man who has pierced the air and penetrated the sky, wended his way amongst the stars and overpassed the margins of the world, who has broken down those imaginary divisions between spheres. . . . He has given eyes to blind moles, and illuminated those who could not see their own image in the innumerable mirrors of reality which surround them on every side; he has loosened the mute tongues which cared little for intricate discussion; he has strengthened the crippled limbs which were too weak to make that journey of the spirit of which base matter is incapable.[11]

This extraordinary passage contains several motifs that deserve attention. Bruno, who understands himself to be a new messiah, claims to have "released the human spirit" and "set knowledge at liberty" and to have "given eyes to blind moles, . . . loosened the mute tongues [and] strengthened the crippled limbs which were too weak to make that journey of the spirit." Moreover, we learn that Bruno's confidence in his ability to carry out his role is based on his conviction that he has made the ascent from the terrestrial through the celestial to the supercelestial, *i.e.,* he has followed the path that Ficino indicates will make man a terrestrial god. In this passage, we also see the sources of the disorder and misunderstanding that plague the world. According to Bruno, the condition is the result of false "Mercuries and Apollos [who] have with many kinds of deceit imposed brutal follies and vices upon the world in the guise of virtues." From other sections of the *Cena* and from his other writ-

11. Bruno, *Dialoghi,* 29–33/Yates, *Giordano Bruno,* 236ff.

ings, it is evident that the reference to Mercury is to the confused and deformed teachings of theology and the reference to Apollo is to the disorder in philosophy.

From this passage and from his previous reference to the significance of Copernicus, we can see that Bruno regards his heliocentric system as heralding "the full sunrise of the ancient and true philosophy after its agelong burial in . . . dark caverns." Later, Bruno indicates that his recovery and promulgation of the Ancient Wisdom can serve as the means for overcoming the present state of personal, social, and political disorder and disorientation.

> [The Ancient Wisdom] produced men who were temperate in their lives, expert in the arts of healing, judicious in contemplation, remarkable in divination, having miraculous powers in magic, wary of superstitions, law-abiding, of irreproachable morality, penetrating in theology, heroic in all their ways. This is shown in the length of their lives, the greater strength of their bodies, their most lofty inventions, their prophecies which have come true; they knew how to transform substances and how to live peacefully in society; their sacraments were inviolable, their executions most just, they were in communion with good and tutelar spirits, and the vestiges of their amazing prowess endure unto this day.[12]

In *Spaccio della bestia trionfante,* Bruno presents a brief mythic description of the end of an age of darkness and the beginning of enlightenment.[13] This text contains a scene in which the celestial powers that control the world convene to remedy the disorder that plagues it. In an elaborate mythic description of a realignment of planetary influences, the celestial powers initiate this plan of action in order to renew or regenerate the creation. Bruno comments that the gods' efforts must be matched by the magus, who can use the new celestial alignments to help usher in the age of regeneration. This text makes clear that the efforts of the magus are essential in overcoming human ignorance and in installing a perfect social order that will end the present state of turmoil.

In addition to searching the heavens for signs of a cosmic re-

12. Bruno, 43–44/Yates, 238ff.
13. This work appeared in 1584. An English translation was prepared by A. D. Imerti, *The Expulsion of the Triumphant Beast* (New Brunswick, N.J., 1964).

vitalization, Bruno also studied the political developments of his time. He was looking for a leader who could pave the way for a universal religious and political reformation. Frances Yates has shown that some of Bruno's travels seem to have been part of that search. He was drawn to England, for example, because of his high regard for the reign of Elizabeth. There is reason to believe that he hoped that she might be able to align herself with the French king Henry III to end the religious wars and bring general political stability to Europe. When circumstances no longer favored Henry III, Bruno transferred his hopes to Henry of Navarre. In fact, according to Yates, it was Bruno's confidence that the accession of Henry IV would lead to a universal European religious and political reformation that prompted him to take the fatal step of returning to Italy.[14]

In the early 1590s, Bruno repeatedly expressed his conviction that he would be the spiritual messiah who would join with political leaders to affect that reformation. Some evidence comes in testimony from those in contact with him during this time. "The prior of the Carmelite monastery at which Bruno stayed in Frankfort . . . [reported] that he was always writing and dreaming and astrologising about new things . . . ; that he said that he knew more than the Apostles, and that, if he had a mind to it, he could bring it about that all the world should be of one religion." When Henry of Navarre defeated the Catholic League and its Spanish backing in 1591, Bruno expected a "universal reform within a Catholic framework." This expectation was reported by an informant testifying against him at the Venetian Inquisition. "[Catholic religion] has need of great reform; it is not good as it is now, but soon the world will see a general reform of itself, for it is impossible that such corruptions should endure; he [Bruno] hopes great things of the King of Navarre, and he means to hurry to publish his works to gain credit in this way, for when the time comes he wishes to be 'capitano' and he will not be always poor for he will enjoy the treasures of others."[15]

Drawing upon the *Sommario* documents of his trial, Yates demonstrates that "the legend that Bruno was prosecuted as a philosophi-

14. Yates, *Giordano Bruno*, 211ff.
15. *Ibid.*, 340f.

cal thinker, was burned for his daring views on innumerable worlds or on the movement of the earth, can no longer stand."[16] It is now clear that Bruno was condemned for his belief that the Egyptian religion was the highest religion given by God, reversing the view of Ficino and others that the ancient theology pointed the way to the fuller revelation of Christianity. Moreover, he understood his mission as one of a religious reformer who would be an instrument in purging the Church and in instituting a new ecumenic religion based on Hermetism and magic.

Bruno, then, provides further evidence of sacralization's mounting criticism of orthodox Christianity and the concurrent search for the means to overcome alienation and install an enduring political order.

CAMPANELLA

The year 1600, because of its numerological combinations of nine and three, signaled for Campanella the beginning of a new age in which the world would be renewed and religious strife and political turmoil put to an end. Like Bruno, Campanella found the key to understanding the unfolding new age in the Hermetic magical teachings. Also, like Bruno, he believed he had a messianic role in ushering in the new age. In 1599, Campanella attempted to establish in Calabria in southern Italy the new capital for worldwide religious and political reform. This rebellion against the Spanish monarchy and the papacy led to an imprisonment that cost him twenty years of his life. It did not, however, destroy his dream of the renewal of society and the world, nor did it diminish his conviction about his signal role. While in prison, Campanella wrote *La Città del Sole*, for which he is best remembered.[17] During this time he also wrote first to the Spanish monarch and then to the pope, describing the "natural" signs that foretold their leading a universal reform that would end the present state of ignorance and alienation. Upon his release

16. *Ibid.*, 355. *Il Sommario del Processo di Giordano Bruno*, a summary of evidence used by the Inquisitors, was discovered in the archives of Pius IX in the 1940s.

17. The edition used is Tommaso Campanella, *La Città del Sole: Dialogo Poetico* [The city of the sun: A poetical dialogue], a bilingual edition prepared by Daniel J. Donno (Berkeley, 1981).

from prison, he went to Rome and was well received by Pope Urban VIII and was even credited with performing astral magic that overcame the hostile configuration threatening the pope's life. Shortly afterward, Campanella went to France, where Louis XIII and Richelieu welcomed him because he proclaimed that the French monarch was to lead the reformation of the world. This analysis will briefly examine Campanella's writings and actions during the critical periods of the Calabrian revolt, his imprisonment, and his journeys to Rome and France.

Campanella made little or no tactical preparation for his Calabrian revolt and gave little consideration to military strategies. Instead, he and his followers, many of whom were Dominicans (as was he), explained to their countrymen the signs revealing that a divinely inspired revolution was to occur. Through his esoteric studies, Campanella found such signs in the heavens, particularly in the sun's moving closer to the earth, and in the numerological significance of the year 1600. After pointing to these signs, Campanella urged his listeners to serve as catalysts for the coming of the new age by freeing themselves from Spanish domination and by installing Campanella as the religious and political leader of the new era. *La Città del Sole* is not a utopia in the often used sense of an idealized, imaginary place free of the problems that plague the real world. It is a description of the state that Campanella had expected to establish in Calabria. If we look briefly at the organization of the City, the skills of its priest-king, and the advantages provided the citizenry, the origin and the ancestry of this new republic become unmistakable.

According to the text, the City was built on a hill surrounded by a vast plain. There were seven circular divisions that corresponded to the seven planets. Four roads crossed the City and followed the points of the compass; they ran from the outer gates to its center. At the very center of the City was a marvelous temple, which was an *omphalos*, a link between the City and the celestial powers that governed it. The altar had a *mappamondo* that depicted all the heavens and another showing all the earth. The ceiling of the dome showed all the great stars, with their names and the powers they have over things below; these representations correspond to the globes on the altar. The temple contained seven lamps named after the seven planets. The walls surrounding the temple were also decorated on both sides. These illustrations serve as an encyclopedia of the accumulated mathematical, geographical, sociological, and philological structure of the world and of its peoples. Also identified were basic geological formations, the vegetative world, the animal world, etc. On the interior of the outmost wall, the mechanical arts and their inventors were displayed, and on the exterior were images of the inventors of sciences and laws including Moses, Osiris, Jupiter, Mercury, Mohammad, and many others. In a high place of honor on this wall were represented Christ and the twelve apostles.[18] Frances Yates rightly notes, "The City was thus a complete reflection of the world as governed by the laws of natural magic in dependence on the stars. The great men were those who had best understood and used those laws, inventors, moral teachers, miracle workers, religious leaders, in short, Magi, of whom the chief was Christ with His apostles." The head of the City was a priest-king who was a master of natural magic.

> [Through his administration] the people of the City lived in brotherly love, having all things in common; they were intelligent and well-educated, the children beginning at an early age to learn all about the world and all arts and sciences from the pictures on the walls. They encouraged scientific invention, all inventions being used in the service of the community to improve the general well-being. They were healthy and well skilled in medicine. And they were virtuous. In this City, the virtues had conquered the vices, for the names of its magistrates were Liberality, Magnanimity, Chastity, Fortitude, Justice. . . . Hence, among the Solarians, there was no robbery, murder, incest, adultery, no malignity or malevolence of any kind.[19]

The head of the City was a magus who could "draw down the life of heaven," as Ficino had described. From our previous analysis, it is clear that Campanella's City is a re-creation of the city of Adocentyn. This re-creation is connected with the passage in the *Asclepius* that

18. Campanella, *Città del Sole*, 27–45. See also Yates, *Giordano Bruno*, 367ff.
19. Yates, *Giordano Bruno*, 369.

prophesied the restoration of the Egyptian religion and law after a time of ignorance and darkness.

During his imprisonment, Campanella also prepared works that prophesied the coming of a universal reform through either the Spanish monarch or the papacy.[20] Moreover, he continued to see this reform occurring through a strengthening of Christianity by Hermetic magic and saw his own role as that of the primary shaper of the program of reform. In each instance, prophecy is of a reform "in which a priesthood of Catholic Magi keep the City in permanent happiness, health and virtue, and the religion of the City is in perfect accord with its scientific view of the world, that is to say with natural magic." Frances Yates aptly describes the consequences of Campanella's efforts. "Campanella's astounding determination and pertinacity gradually had their reward; the monarchs of the world began to take an interest in the prisoner, and the man who, in 1599, had gone into prison in imminent danger of death for dangerous heresies and revolt against Spain was, in 1626, released from prison through Spanish influence."[21]

Two episodes in Campanella's career following his release deserve special attention. The first is his performing anti-eclipse magic for Pope Urban VIII.[22] The pope was greatly troubled by astrological forecasts of imminent death. By 1628, rumors became loud and widespread, no doubt encouraged by the Spanish, who were annoyed by his consistently pro-French policy. The two dangerous years were 1628, when there was an eclipse of the moon in January and of the sun in December, and 1630, when there was another solar eclipse in June. There are records that show that the pope and Campanella frequently conferred on the meanings of these astrological events and the prophylactic measures that could be taken against them. Campanella's own records indicate that he constructed what was in effect a model of the cosmos that could draw

20. References are made in Tommaso Campanella, *Monarchia di Spagna* (1620) and *Monarchia Messiae* (1633).

21. Yates, *Giordano Bruno*, 386f.

22. For a fuller discussion of these events, see Walker, *Spiritual and Demonic Magic*, Chap. 7, which is the principal source of this analysis.

the beneficial powers from appropriate planets and, therefore, correct the misalignment in the heavens themselves. These efforts on the pope's behalf gained Campanella sufficient favor that he was permitted to establish a college in Rome for the training of missionaries who would convert the whole world to Campanella's kind of Catholicism.[23]

By 1634, Campanella was again out of favor. Undaunted, however, he transferred his ministrations to the French monarchy. Shortly after his arrival in Paris, Campanella had published or circulated in manuscript form his analysis of the astrological evidence that the power of the Spanish monarchy was weakening while that of the French monarchy was growing. In fact, Louis XIII was to be the new Charlemagne who would free Europe from Spanish tyranny. Moreover, the Paris edition of *La Città del Sole* linked his vision of the utopian reform directly to the French monarchy. The most intriguing episode in his stay in France, however, occurred in 1638, when the son of Louis XIII was born. Campanella prepared a commemorative eclogue. It was consistent with his vision of the French monarchy's restoration of universal harmony and was modeled on Virgil's famous Fourth Eclogue. Campanella begins with the astrological signs that show that a renewal of the world is at hand and that a new reign of religious vitality and social tranquillity is about to begin. Campanella then refers to the dauphin as the "French Cock destined to rule with a reformed Peter a united world. In this coming dispensation, labour will be a pleasure amicably shared by all; all will recognize one God and Father and love will unite all; all kings and peoples will assemble in a city which they will call Héliaca, the City of the Sun, which will be built by this illustrious hero."[24] It is evidently from this reference that Louis XIV gained the title le Roi Soleil.

These events in Rome and in Paris in the last part of Campanella's life mark the full emergence of the Hermetic sacralizing tradition. In the Hermetic materials themselves and in Ficino's description of man's powers as a terrestrial god, there is a presentation of man as master of the forces that shape his destiny. In the account of Campanella and Urban VIII, we see a magus using his knowledge not only to draw the beneficial powers from the heavens but, in fact, to create an alternate model that can correct an actual disorder. With Campanella, too, the emphasis on the magus as the creator of the perfect social order emerges completely. In the idealized city of Hermes, all human physical, emotional, and spiritual needs were met through the efforts of the magus. Campanella's efforts, similarly, are directed at the institution or, more accurately, the reinstitution of a perfect society.

Campanella's eclogue to Louis XIV is particularly significant in the history of modern political thought, for it provides a compact, vivid expression of a Kingdom of God on earth. Two other major political motifs are well-known elements of sixteenth- and seventeenth-century thought. There was first of all the yearning for the reinstitution of a Christian ecumenic empire that would overcome the religious and political fractures plaguing Europe. This tradition dates back to the beginning of the Holy Roman Empire and continues in the legends of Italy, Germany, France, and England. The second motif, expressed in Virgil's eclogue, envisions the founding of an empire that will bring an end to turmoil and create an age of peace and prosperity. This image, revived by the Latin humanists, was held as the secular alternative to the vision of a Christian empire. But Campanella provides a third image—a perfectly ordered state developed through the recovery of the Ancient Wisdom, particularly Hermetic magic. Of the three of these, Campanella's is most closely connected to the features of modernity. It characterizes the current state of Christianity as corrupted and disordered and scorns its pretensions to wisdom. It sees, however, a new age of enlightenment in which man gains unprecedented knowledge, which restores man to his true nature and overcomes his fundamental alienation. As a result, man is able to recognize his true nature, discover his dignity, and institute a harmonious social order free from corruption and immorality.

The recognition of this third utopian image helps to explain connections that Löwith and Voegelin have explored between the religious traditions and the modern progressivist constructions of history. The fundamental problem is that these analyses require that a radical Christian dualism become an immanentist construction. Blumenberg and others have criticized this transformation because the Christian Kingdom of God fundamentally differs from the descriptions of a perfect society on earth. Moreover, Blumenberg also challenged scholars to demonstrate the historical steps in such a transformation. The development of the sacralizing pattern, particularly the emphasis on social and political reformation, during the sixteenth and seventeenth centuries supplies part of the evidence. It shares modernity's criticism of the Christian "dark age" and its yearning for a new political order. These parallels can be further demonstrated in the work of Bacon, Comte, and Marx; and this analysis, in turn, poses further questions about conventional interpretations of modernity as the result of secularization.

Chapter Five

BACON, COMTE, AND MARX: A REVALUATION

This reconsideration of key elements in the work of Bacon, Comte, and Marx demonstrates parallels between their writings and the sacralizing pattern. It must be emphasized that this analysis does not attempt to discredit or disregard secularizing patterns within their writings. Rather, the purpose is to show that there are additional sacralizing influences that affect their formulations of a new epistemology and a new program of social reformation.

There are several reasons for choosing these three. The first is that each writer's work displays the three primary characteristics of modernity: the consciousness of an epochal break with the past; a conviction that this break is due to an epistemological advance; and the belief that this new knowledge provides man the means of overcoming his alienation and regaining his true humanity. In addition to sharing these general features, each man's work has distinctive elements that we want to consider in light of the new understanding of the sacralizing pattern. Bacon, for example, has long been regarded as the father of the scientific method. For this reason he has enjoyed a place of honor as a leader in the seventeenth-century battle of the ancients and the moderns. We now want to revaluate Bacon's celebrated program for the advancement of learning and to determine the extent to which his great instauration is drawn from the principles of empirical science. Through this analysis, we intend to examine connections between Bacon's utopian vision of a new Atlantis and the myths and symbols of the sacralizing tradition.

Comte is of course known as the father of social science. His work includes not only an epistemology that attempts to emulate the empirical sciences but also a program of social reformation that is supposed to install a perfect social order. Again, without denying the influence of natural science, we will examine the influence of esoteric religion and pseudo-science on his program. The reconsideration of Marx will concentrate on his criticisms of traditional philosophy and religion, his concept of alienation, and his vision of social and political life after the Communist Revolution. The intent is to develop parallels between these elements of Marxist thought and main elements of the sacralizing tradition, especially the utopian programs of the sixteenth and seventeenth centuries.

BACON

Bacon's reputation in the eighteenth and nineteenth centuries as the patriarch of the modern age is certainly understandable. He, more than any other seventeenth-century thinker, led the attack on traditional learning and developed a thorough overhaul of the premises of philosophical and scientific inquiry. In addition to his theoretical work, he helped create a new scientific society (the Royal Society) to advance the understanding of the natural world and enhance the development of technology and the mechanical arts. Moreover, in laying the groundwork for a new form of scholarly collaboration, he set forth some of the most basic guidelines for scientific research, e.g., the sharing of theories and experimental results on an international basis and the testing of theories through independent experimental verification.

It was for these contributions that Bacon was recognized as a leader in the great battle of the modernists against the ancients. A brief analysis will show, however, that Bacon's break with the ancient traditions is not as clear-cut as has been claimed. In fact, his criticisms of philosophy and theology and his proposals for a thoroughgoing social reformation closely parallel the main elements of the sacralizing pattern found in the Ancient Wisdom. Of course, this analysis does not intend to deny or to discredit Bacon's contributions to the advancement of science and technology. It does, however, seek to demonstrate that these advances develop hand in hand with a dream of innerworldly perfection that is deeply rooted in the sacralizing tradition.

This brief examination concentrates on two of Bacon's principal works, *The Advancement of Learning* (1605) and *The New Atlantis* (1627).[1] The main lines of *The Advancement of Learning* are generally known. In it Bacon criticizes the disorder and confusion of the various scholarly traditions and urges a fundamental reform so that man can gain an accurate knowledge of the natural world and use his knowledge to improve the human condition. The book is dedicated to James I because Bacon hopes that the king will recognize the national importance of encouraging the development of new disciplines as a counter to the muddled teaching going on in the universities. Bacon's vision of the social benefits to be gained from the reform and the advancement of learning is presented in his later work, *The New Atlantis*. In order to establish the connections between this utopia and Bacon's analytical works, such as *The Advancement of Learning*, we need to summarize the plot.[2]

A European ship, off course, happens onto an unknown and uncharted territory, Ben Salem or The New Atlantis. The Europeans are hospitably received into the city and are fascinated to find that the inhabitants live in contentment and happiness, having their material, emotional, and spiritual needs completely satisfied. Of course, these conditions stand in contrast to the disorder and disarray in Europe. When the Europeans express their admiration to the

1. The standard editions of both texts are found in Francis Bacon, *Works*, ed. James Spedding, R. L. Ellis, and D. D. Heath (14 vols.; London, 1857–74). *The Advancement of Learning* appears in Vol. II and *The New Atlantis* in Vol. III.

2. This summary and parts of this analysis follow closely Frances Yates, "Francis Bacon 'Under the Shadow of Jehova's Wings,'" in Yates, *The Rosicrucian Enlightenment* (London, 1972), 118–29. Also pertinent is Yates's essay "The Hermetic Tradition in Renaissance Science," in C. S. Singleton (ed.), *Art, Science, and History in the Renaissance* (Baltimore, 1967), 255–74. Also, this study is indebted to Paolo Rossi, *Francesco Bacone: dalla magia alla scienza* (Bari, 1957), translated by Sacha Rabinovitch as *Francis Bacon: From Magic to Science* (Chicago, 1968).

leaders of the city and their anxiousness to learn the secret, they are told that the leaders know that the fundamental problem is the confused and distorted understanding of reality that prevails in Europe. When the Europeans appeal to the Ben Salemites for the true understanding of reality that will allow them to reform their own world, the leaders readily agree to teach them.

From this brief account, we recognize the now-familiar criticism of the derailment of learning that results in man's fundamental alienation from his true nature and a consequent breakdown of social and political order. Of course, this theme can be found in programs of religious reformation and secularization as well as in the sacralizing tradition. However, an examination of the root images in Bacon's utopia and in his other writings makes clear that they belong to the sacralizing pattern. In *The Advancement of Learning*, there are extended criticisms of the derailment of knowledge by classical philosophy and subsequently by Christian theology, which has adopted these principles and become contaminated by them. Bacon's title *The New Atlantis* seems intended to recall the Platonic myth of the city of Atlantis, and the purpose of this allusion is to permit the description of the human condition prior to the disorder and disorientation engineered by philosophy. The intent of this remythologizing seems comparable to Agrippa's reinterpretation of Adam's sin as the source of man's alienation. In fact, Bacon elsewhere traces man's alienation back to a similar reinterpretation of Adam's sin.[3] Implicit in these mythic references is the conviction that this alienation can be overcome and man can regain his true destiny. From both *The Advancement of Learning* and *The New Atlantis*, it is evident that Bacon's understanding of man's true nature is similar to the mythic description in the sacralizing tradition of man as a terrestrial god possessing the knowledge to control nature and to perfect society. These parallels become clearer and more substantial in a close consideration of themes and images in *The New Atlantis*. When the travelers arrive, their sick are cared for in the Strangers' House; when they offer payment, it is refused. Shortly afterward a city official comes for a visit, wearing a white turban

---

3. See the preface to Francis Bacon, *Instauratio Magna*, in *Works*, I, 132f. For a detailed discussion of this theme, see Rossi, *Francis Bacon*, 128ff.

with a small red cross on the top. Later the governor visits them and describes in detail the House of Salomon, which is the college of wise men who are both priests and political leaders. When the strangers ask how the Ben Salemites know the affairs of the outside world so completely, the reply is that members of the city regularly go abroad disguised in the dress of the country visited. Their purpose is to try to find like-minded people drawn to the light of knowledge that the Ben Salemites seek to spread throughout the world.[4]

Before the Europeans disembark, an official gives them a scroll of instructions. "This scroll was signed with a stamp of cherubin's wings, not spread, but hanging downwards, and by them a cross."[5] These specific details show how closely Bacon's utopia draws upon Rosicrucian myths and symbols. That tradition amalgamates the Hermetic and Cabalist traditions of the Renaissance magicians with alchemy and with mystical Christianity. Although these new elements contribute new myths and symbols, the fundamental features of the Rosicrucian tradition adhere to the sacralizing pattern as developed here. And they reflect a yearning for recovery from the spiritual, intellectual, and political disorder of the age; the hope is for a religious-political leader.[6] The references noted in *The New Atlantis* are characteristic of the Rosicrucian movement. The scroll with the cherubin's wings and the cross, for example, is a prime emblem. Also, the Rosicrucians were specifically charged to heal the sick gratis. The most explicit connection is the red cross worn by officials of new Atlantis. Another basic element of Bacon's thought that he shares with the Rosicrucian tradition is that they prophesied the dawn of a new age in which Adam's sin would be overcome and man's true nature restored.

There are several reasons for making this connection. First, it establishes parallels between Bacon's criticism of the deterioration of learning and the coming of a new age of knowledge. While there are several sources for this tradition, Bacon's work is directly and specifically related to sacralization. His vision of social reformation

4. See Yates, *Rosicrucian Enlightenment*, 126ff., for a more detailed description and analysis.
5. Bacon, *Works*, III, 130. Also see Yates, *Rosicrucian Enlightenment*, 126ff.
6. See Yates, *Rosicrucian Enlightenment*, passim.

through a recovery of esoteric knowledge uses the themes and imagery found in the work of Agrippa and Bruno and adds the
Rosicrucian alchemical imagery. A fundamental contention of this
study has been that the characteristic features of modern consciousness are shaped by a sacralizing as well as a secularizing tradition. We find in Bacon specific evidence: Not only are the general
features of his program for the advancement of learning, which
leads to a new Atlantis, those of the sacralizing tradition, the specific
details are drawn from its myths and symbols.
It is important to be clear on the point being made. The evidence
of this influence does not undercut or diminish Bacon's contributions to the development of the scientific method or to the founding
of the Royal Society. Nor does it diminish or discredit the elements
of his revisions that draw upon the inductive and experimental
principles of seventeenth-century science. Instead, the point is that
science was not completely differentiated from the general philosophical and religious climate of the sixteenth and seventeenth
centuries. Europe was in convulsions from a religious upheaval and
from ever-changing political realignments. The basic yearning in the
sixteenth century for a reconciliation and a reordering of society was
still very much alive in Bacon's age and, for that matter, in the
eighteenth century as well. What we find in Bacon's work is another
expression of this fundamental longing. He has incorporated elements from science, but his scientific principles are integrated into
the myths, symbols, and the basic yearnings expressed in the sacralizing tradition. Moreover, Frances Yates has shown that the
Rosicrucian tradition tended to appropriate elements of science into
the magical and alchemical materials as another resource for transforming the conditions of existence.
Conventional treatments of Bacon are therefore inaccurate and
inadequate when they seek to make him a pioneer who completely
abandoned traditional philosophy and pseudo-science for the new
science. There is in his work a compact intermingling of science, an
early form of positivism, mystical religion, pseudo-science, and
classical mythology and fables. The controlling myths and metaphors that give shape to Bacon's enterprise, however, are primarily
those of the sacralizing tradition that depict man as a terrestrial god.

This transformation restores man to his full humanity and overcomes the alienation that has plagued him through most of his history. As we shall see, this basic pattern continues in the development of social science in the work of Comte and Marx. While their work, like Bacon's, attempts to establish new epistemological principles based on the natural sciences, the basic conviction about the results to be obtained from this epistemological shift, however, is found in the sacralizing tradition and not in science or secularization.[7]

COMTE

Comte's signal contribution to modern thought is found in his creation of social science (*physique sociale*), positivist philosophy, and his famous three-stage progressivist construction of history. He is regarded as a secularist because he argues that theology and metaphysics represent the childhood and adolescent phases in the development of Western rationalism and because he asserts that man regains his dignity and self-determination by ridding himself of the oppressive delusion of God. Without attempting to deny these elements of Comte's position, we intend to revaluate the foundations of his programs for epistemological and social reformation in light of what we now know about the sacralizing tradition.

This brief treatment cannot cover the range of issues raised in Comte's writings. Instead, the examination can consider only three concerns that occupied Comte's attention from his earliest writings to the last. The first is his program of epistemological reformation; the second is his plan to create a new social order; and the third is his proposal to establish a new religion of humanity. His two major works, *Cours de philosophie positive* (1830–42), and *Système de politique*

7. For a current treatment that takes an alternate view of Bacon, especially of *The Advancement of Learning*, see Jerry Weinberger, *Science, Faith and Politics: Francis Bacon and the Utopian Roots of the Modern Age* (Ithaca, 1985). Weinberger's purpose is to "restore the now-forgotten eighteenth century view that Francis Bacon was the greatest of all the 'moderns' . . . who recommended turning the human intellect from the contemplation of God and nature to the scientific project for mastering nature and fortune" (9). Despite the difference in interpretation, Weinberger's analysis nevertheless confirms my treatment of Bacon's utopian vision as a key component of the modern age.

positive (1851–54), and his correspondence with friends and colleagues will be considered.[8]

Cours sets out his critique of the state of the various disciplines and contains his call to abandon theological and metaphysical speculations as useless and counterproductive. He also proposes a new philosophy that discards metaphysical inquiries into origins or purpose and concentrates on phenomena as they are known through the laws of nature and as they contribute to the welfare of humanity.[9] This element of his work is responsible for his reputation as one of the great modernists. His criticism of metaphysics as a garbled and jumbled mess resulting from the confusion of theology with classical philosophy and his consequent proposal to model all knowledge upon the principles of the natural sciences are a systematic statement of the spirit of the modern age.

The new age of positivism is to be advanced by two developments that follow from the new epistemology. The first is a thorough reformation of the educational system aimed at public school and university curricula. Also, for the less well educated, it proposes revisions in popular sources of information such as the calendar and various social rituals that identify the principal events and the most important leaders in the new age.[10] That age itself is to be installed through the emergence of a new intellectual class with Comte as its leader. This class will contain those who have mastered the principles of science and who can apply them to both the natural and the social sciences. These intellectuals are to supervise the technologists who actually implement the various programs of applied science, which range from agriculture to medicine and economics.[11]

8. There is no critical edition of Comte's works. There is a condensed, two-volume English translation of the six volumes of the *Cours* by Harriet Martineau that was personally approved by Comte. Also, a full English translation of the *Système* by J. H. Bridges *et al.* was published as *System of Positive Polity* (4 vols.; London, 1875–77). For scholarly works pertinent to this discussion, see the bibliographical listings under "Comte."

9. The sections of the *Cours* most pertinent to this discussion are the Préliminaires Généraux, Chaps. 1 and 2, and Book VI, "Physique Sociale," esp. Chaps. 1, 3, 6, and 15.

10. See Comte, *Cours*, esp. the Préliminaires Généraux; Comte, *Système*, Vol. IV, Chaps. 2 and 5.

11. See Comte, *Système*, Vol. I, Introduction Fondamentale, and Chaps. 1 and 2.

The second development integral to the installation of the new age is an overhaul of religion.[12] Comte rejects Protestant and Catholic theology because both are sources of man's alienation from himself. By positing a transcendent Creator who sits in judgment, theology has fundamentally impeded man's realization of his full potential. Comte proposes as an alternative the religion of humanity. He is to be the pontiff of a church hierarchy that establishes the basic scriptures and creeds to guide people to the truth. Through this process of regular participation in religious practice, the masses will be able to overcome the disorientation caused by "the great malady," *i.e.*, theism, and mankind will be led toward the recovery of its true nature.

These basic features of Comte's work should by now suggest connections with the sacralizing tradition. First, there is the familiar criticism that the present intellectual disorientation stems from traditional theology and philosophy. There is also the characteristic expectation of a breakthrough in man's understanding of himself and of the world. This new epistemological leap, in turn, serves as the basis for a reformation of man's understanding of himself and of society. Moreover, if we compare his program to Bacon's new Atlantis, we see additional connections with the utopian dreams inspired by the sacralizing tradition. In Comte's new society, scientists and priests have an encyclopedic knowledge of the natural world and of human nature, and they are able to master nature, to reform religion, and to perfect society. Consequently, they can direct the individual and society toward meaning, purpose, and fulfillment. Moreover, as the priest-philosopher and political leader of this group, Comte seems very much in the tradition of the first great magus, Hermes Trismegistus. To a great degree, Comte's program aims at creating a society much like Adocentyn or the new Atlantis. Bacon had put the new Atlantis far away in space. Comte, even more sure about the coming reformation, locates the new society in Europe and in the immediate future.

From the outset, this revaluation has insisted that it does not propose to introduce sacralizing elements in order to exclude secu-

---

12. *Ibid.*, Vol. I, Introduction Fondamentale, and Chap. 6, "Instituant la religion de l'Humanité," and Vol. IV, Chaps. 1 and 2, and the "Calendrier Positiviste."

larizing patterns. At the same time, it is important to note that some elements considered to be characteristically secular take on new dimensions in light of what we now know of the sacralizing tradition. Consider, for example, the notion of a positive philosophy that abandons the theological and metaphysical quest for origins. On the surface, this seems quite different from the esoteric search for the definitive answers to how and why the world was created. Nevertheless, there are fundamental connections. For Comte and for the magus, the ultimate epistemological issue centers on the knowledge that allows man to control the natural world and shape his own destiny. How the world operates is more important than is the question of origins. Or, perhaps more accurately, the question of origins is important only in relation to the question of operation. Moreover, there is a sense in which the lack of interest in origins also reflects a concept of human nature closely related to the sacralizing tradition. The question is ultimately aimed at determining man's place in the hierarchy of being and is the query of a creature rather than a creator. When man understands himself to be the creator and shaper of his own destiny, the question of origins becomes relatively insignificant. As a terrestrial god, man is more concerned with shaping the future than with knowing the past.

In order to clarify further this association between Comte and the sacralists, we can contrast his views to the secularizing pattern found in Boccaccio and Machiavelli. Boccaccio, as a secularist, sees a fundamental gulf between secular affairs and God. He does not deny the reality of God, but God's plan and purpose are finally unknowable. Hence man is alone in this world to contend with Fortune and Necessity. Similarly, Machiavelli completely disregards references to a transcendent, sacred source of man's destiny. Man must shape his own destiny as he contends with Fortune and Necessity. The fundamental difference between these secularists and Comte is that they see the world as controlled by unpredictable, capricious forces that man cannot know or control but must nevertheless contend with insofar as humanly possible. Comte, on the other hand, believes that the forces operating in the world can be known, and this knowledge can be used to control nature and to transform the human condition. Using this knowledge, man can create a perfect social order—a prospect that neither Boccaccio nor Machiavelli could entertain as a possibility.

But is not Comte's rejection of Christian theology a major difference between his position and the sacralizing pattern? Not necessarily, for the later Renaissance magi rejected traditional Christianity, and Comte's reasons are similar to theirs. Comte believes that it is a misleading pseudo-religion. Similarly, Bruno sees the Egyptian religion, or Hermetism, as the source for a correction of religion led astray by Christianity.

Comte's failure to recognize Christ as the true messiah also has its precedent in the sacralizing tradition. During his trial, Bruno indicated that he did not believe that Jesus was the source of the ultimate revelation from God, and Campanella had Christ in a place of honor among several other magi. So the Christocentrism of orthodox theology was greatly diminished in the Renaissance sacralizing tradition. But there is a more significant connection between Comte and the Renaissance magi. Each regarded himself as a messianic figure bringing new light into an age of darkness. This view was especially pronounced in both Bruno and in Campanella. Comte, as the messiah of a new age, also denied that the revelation in Christ was definitive. In fact, it was for him a spiritual derailment.

Finally, what is to be said about the radical emphasis on a new religion of humanity rather than on a religion devoted to God? This position obviously is in stark contrast to the theological and metaphysical traditions that Comte criticizes. It is not so far removed, however, from the sacralizing tradition, which has as its fundamental focus the recovery of man's full human capacity as a terrestrial god. In the sixteenth and early seventeenth centuries, this tradition grew apart from Christianity to the point that it increasingly criticized the derailments within the Christian tradition that caused a fundamental misunderstanding of man's nature and his place in the world. Comte's religion of humanity shares this view. In fact, its correspondence with this tradition is easier to see than is trying to explain Comte's new religion in light of the secularizing tradition as represented in the works of Boccaccio and Machiavelli.

Comte is different from the early sacralizers in that he belongs with the moderns in the ancients-and-moderns controversy. Like

Bacon, he emphasizes science rather than the earlier pseudo-sciences. Nevertheless, science functions in the same way the pseudo-sciences did during the fifteenth and sixteenth centuries. It provides the means for transforming human nature, and it is directly associated with both a religious renewal and a social reformation. Moreover, there is the tie with the seventeenth-century utopian views of science as a powerful form of instrumental knowledge that could control nature and could perfect society. In fact, Comte links science with his sacralizing project even more strongly than did some of the earlier utopian writers. Science is the principal component of a new revelation to be communicated through the organs of the church organization and the ritual practices of religion. With this new religious truth, care must be taken to establish its fundamental core and to guard against error. For the most part, this new truth has to be promulgated this way because the ignorant are incapable of discovering it themselves. Therefore, Comte's religion of humanity, with its basis in science, is very close to the conventional view of the Church as the recipient of the highest revelation, which must be made palatable to the masses so they can be saved.

In summary, then, Comte's work appears to be more closely aligned to the sacralizing than to the secularizing tradition. It retains a fundamental religious thrust, though it is an immanent rather than a transcendent religion. Moreover, its view of human nature depicts man as a being with a godlike capacity to control nature and shape his own destiny. Marx, on the other hand, completely rejects religion as a principal source and form of alienation. Nevertheless, his concepts of human nature and society closely parallel those of the Renaissance magi.

MARX

The purpose of this analysis is to demonstrate that conventional interpretations of Marx as a secularizer must now be reassessed.[13] The intent of this call for a revaluation, however, is not to substitute one monochromatic interpretation for another. There obviously are components of Marxist thought that are influenced by seculariza-

13. For the scholarly works used in this analysis, see the bibliographical entries under "Marx."

tion. Still others are not shaped by either of these ideological frameworks but emerge from a sound empirical analysis of social and economic conditions in the mid-nineteenth century. No single mode of interpretation, therefore, can account for all the main currents in Marx's treatment of economics, society, and history. It is equally important to recognize, however, that some interpretive modes are more directly relevant to certain aspects of Marxism than are others. The specific premise that follows from this general observation is that comparisons with the sacralizing tradition are the most effective means of understanding Marxism's criticisms of traditional philosophy and religion, its description of man's alienation from his full humanity, and the utopian character of Marx's "true communism."

The critique of philosophy and religion is a theme that runs throughout Marx's writings. In his doctoral dissertation on Democritus, for example, he criticizes traditional philosophy's contemplative, passive acceptance of the human condition and calls for a new active philosophy that takes Prometheus as its patron saint.[14] Prometheus, the mythical "hater of the gods," steals their fire and gives it to man. This gift is, first of all, symbolic of the civilizational resources and skills man needs to alter the given conditions of existence to suit him. Second, it represents a new autonomy for man—a break from dependence on the gods. The most famous and concise statement of the intention of Marx's Promethean man is in the eleventh thesis on Feuerbach: "Philosophers have only *interpreted* the world; the goal, however, is to *change* it."[15] Marx's reference to Prometheus is reminiscent of Bacon's new Atlantis. Through this symbolism, Bacon contrasted the period of classical philosophy as a time of darkness with the preceding mythical age of light in which man was in possession of the operative knowledge that made him into a magus and a terrestrial god.

The attack on religion is similar to Marx's complaints about tradi-

14. Karl Marx, *Ueber die differenz der demokritischen und epikureischen Naturphilosophie* (1841); *Karl Marx, Friedrich Engels: Historisch-kritische Gesamtausgabe, Werke, Schriften, Briefe,* ed. D. Rjazanov [pseud.] (6 vols.; Frankfurt am Main, 1927–32), I, 85.

15. "Ad Feuerbach," in *Gesamtausgabe,* V, 533–35. English translation from *Basic Writings on Politics and Philosophy [by] Karl Marx and Friedrich Engels,* ed. Lewis S. Feuer (Garden City, N.Y., 1959), 245.

tional philosophy. In several essays he applauds Feuerbach's analysis of its alienating and disorienting effects.[16] Feuerbach's revolutionary position stands the traditional view of Western ethical monotheism on its head. The conventional view attributes the advances in man's moral and intellectual developments to progressive advances in the evolution of religion from primitive polytheism to Judaeo-Christian ethical monotheism. Feuerbach, however, sees this development as man's progressive alienation from his true nature. An increasing sense of man's sinfulness, finitude, and helplessness grew concomitantly with the concept of God as a righteous judge and savior. For Feuerbach, this religious consciousness was false and transferred all of man's innate noble qualities to a transcendent judge and redeemer, leaving man a frail, self-loathing creature. Recovery of man's full humanity required the reintegration of those noble attributes. Building upon Feuerbach's diagnosis and prescription, Marx argued that man must cast off the creaturely consciousness of the Judaeo-Christian tradition. Man must realize that he is the creator of his own destiny.

The attack on religion, then, is similar to the critique of philosophy. Marx regards both as sources of a debilitating misconception of man's nature that emasculates him and leaves him passive and dependent on imaginary forces outside himself. Marx's call for the elimination of traditional philosophy and the Judaeo-Christian religion, therefore, has the fundamental purpose of restoring man to his primary role as the active creator and shaper of his own destiny.[17]

Marx's critiques have close affinities with Agrippa's and Bacon's criticisms of traditional philosophy and religion and with Ficino's and Pico's new understanding of human nature. These parallels become more evident when an analysis is made of the connections between Marx's dream of restoring man's humanity and the goals of

16. In addition to the "Theses on Feuerbach," see, for example, the section on Feuerbach in *The German Ideology,* ed. R. Pascal (1947; rpr. New York, 1968).

17. "The task of history . . . is to establish the truth of this world. The task of philosophy . . . is to unmask self-alienation in its unholy forms. Thus the criticism of heaven turns into the criticism of the earth, the criticism of religion into the criticism of right and the criticism of theology into the criticism of politics" (Karl Marx, "Toward the Critique of Hegel's Philosophy of Right," in *Basic Writings,* 262).

his Communist Revolution. The key to understanding this connection is found in contrasts Marx makes between "crude communism" and "true communism" and between "utopian communism" and "scientific communism."[18]

Marx distinguishes the objectives of crude and true communism in *The German Ideology*.[19] Non-Marxist crude communism has as its goal the improvement of the material conditions under which a worker must earn his living. True communism, on the other hand, seeks to restore man's humanity, which has been lost in the exploitive conditions under which he has been forced to work. In *The Communist Manifesto*, Marx offers a concise contrast between his scientific communism and what he calls utopian communism. Here the basic contrast is not in the goal but in the mode of attaining that goal. Utopian communism proposes to eliminate the prevailing economic conditions and modes of production by returning to a premodern economic system and stage of craftsmanship. Although Marx finds the intent admirable, *viz.*, eliminating the cause of man's alienation from meaningful creative work, he finds the prescription naïve, unhistorical, and unscientific. Marx proposes to use the bourgeois achievements as the instruments of the proletariat's liberation. In fact, Marx insists that the prospects for man overcoming his alienation and attaining his full humanity are directly connected to the extraordinary bourgeois advances in science, technology, and industry. These developments hold the promise of surmounting traditional hardships and drudgery in the struggle for material necessities. Man can then devote his creative energies to a wide range of aesthetic, social, and humanitarian objectives.

One other basic contrast between Marx's communism and other programs of social reformation is important to note. In *The Communist Manifesto* and elsewhere, Marx claims that communism will ultimately succeed where other programs of reformation fail because its basis is his scientific analysis of the material forces controlling the course of society and history. In the *Manifesto* he specifically identifies the turning point in human history as the stage at which intellectuals (namely, himself) discover the course of history and

18. See the section "True Communism," in *The German Ideology*, 79ff.
19. This discussion is based on Voegelin, *From Enlightenment to Revolution*, 290ff.

join the agents of historical change (the proletariat) to direct the action that will usher in the new age of man.[20] In other words, Marx claims that his intellectual endeavors are able to bring enlightenment and to direct humanity toward recovery from the alienated condition that has plagued man throughout history. Marx's conviction that he has reached an unprecedented understanding of the human condition and can employ instrumental knowledge to reshape the conditions of existence, as we shall see, has close connections with the dreams and ambitions of the Renaissance magi. Let us set this in context by returning to Marx's criticism of traditional philosophy and religion. Although he has a reputation as a secularizer, these criticisms actually correspond more closely to the sacralizing pattern.

From the time of Ficino onward, the sacralizing tradition was associated with efforts to reform the understanding of reality propounded in conventional theology and philosophy. Some aimed at renewing and revitalizing Christianity; others—for example, Agrippa and Bruno—sought to correct the derailments brought on by Christianity and its merger with classical philosophy. Marx criticizes traditional philosophy because it stresses contemplation and acceptance of the world. Against that position, Marx wants to present an active merger of theory and practice that will allow man to change the conditions of his existence. This basic characteristic of the sacralizing tradition was first introduced by Ficino in his reconceptualization of magic as the highest form of natural philosophy. This reconceptualization, in turn, was the foundation of his new understanding that links operative knowledge with the power for self-determination, and this concept becomes part of the works of the major figures in the sacralizing tradition from the fifteenth century forward.

Marx's rejection of Christianity also closely parallels the criticisms by Agrippa, Bruno, and other sacralists who regard it as having alienated man from his most noble attributes and robbed him of his

20. Marx states that "a portion of the bourgeois ideologists, who have raised themselves to the level of comprehending theoretically the historical movement as a whole" join the proletariat and organize it into a universal movement "when the class struggle nears the decisive hour" (*The Communist Manifesto*, in *Basic Writings*, 17).

capacity for self-determination. As Marx himself indicates, his hero is Prometheus, who transforms the human condition by giving man resources that had belonged exclusively to the gods. Marx's argument throughout is that man must be self-reliant and self-determining; he cannot be dependent on anything else. These points bring to mind Ficino's description of man as a terrestrial god who resents indebtedness to any being because man is ultimately like God and is, therefore, self-creating. The Marxist view of man also recalls Ficino's argument that man demonstrates his sovereignty as a terrestrial god through his various scientific and technological achievements, *e.g.*, medicine, farming, and engineering.

There are also affinities in the emphasis on knowledge as a means of controlling nature and perfecting society. From the original Hermetic materials through the revival in the fifteenth and sixteenth centuries, power to control nature and to perfect society is associated with an epistemological linking of theoretical and instrumental knowledge. Marx's true communism also shares the Hermetic utopian dream of meeting fundamental physical and material needs through applied knowledge.

Marx apparently differs from the early sacralizers in that he seems to share the secularist's commitment to the new sciences rather than the old pseudo-sciences as the source for regeneration of man. We have seen, however, that the relation of science to pseudo-science in the utopian dreams of world reformation is not as clear and simple as modernists have claimed. With Bacon, for example, the new science is effectively part of the epistemological breakthrough that provides the means for mastering nature and perfecting society. The instrumental means do change, but not the dream of human perfection through knowledge that is basic to the sacralizing tradition. So, again, the claim to use science does not in itself make an effort secular (or scientific). The function of science is the key issue; and in the case of Bacon, Comte, and Marx, we see that science functions as the new and improved version of the old pseudo-science.

Another correlation between the Marxian project and the sacralizing tradition is in the purpose and goal of the Communist Revolution. Marx makes very clear his purpose to overcome man's alienation and restore man to his true humanity. This liberation means that man can use his instrumental and theoretical knowledge to be whatever he wishes to be. This corresponds closely to the Hermetic yearning to make man a terrestrial god. The Marxist view here contrasts sharply with the secularist views of Boccaccio and Machiavelli. For them, man is an active shaper of his life. But Fortune and Necessity mean that man is not in control, that man is not self-determining.

Finally, there is an important parallel between the role of the Hermetic magus and the role Marx proposes to play in the revolution. Marx possesses profound knowledge of the forces governing nature and society, through which he expects to be able to liberate man from his alienation and to perfect society. This is the basic role of the magus in the Hermetic tradition. The magus is the one who combines the knowledge of nature with the transformation of man in this world, and that is Marx's ultimate goal.[21]

21. For an intriguing discussion of Faustian sorcery in Marx by a Marxist, see Marshall Berman, *All That Is Solid Melts into Air: The Experience of Modernity* (New York, 1982).

Conclusion

THE SACRALIZING TRADITION IN THE MODERN AGE

The historical insights and the theoretical developments of recent Renaissance scholarship demonstrate the need for a reconsideration of the origins of modernity and the forces shaping it. More particularly, these studies make it evident that conventional treatments of modernity and secularization must be supplemented and revised in light of the opposite yet complementary influence of sacralization.

The theoretical and empirical basis for this reconceptualization derives from a distinction that needs to be made regarding the Renaissance revival of ancient learning. In addition to the humanist revival of the *studia humanitatis,* the Neoplatonists rediscovered the *prisca theologia.* These materials, which were regarded as the earliest and purest non-Christian revelations, led Ficino and his followers to a new understanding of human nature. *Sacralization* is the term used to characterize this view of man as a terrestrial god capable of controlling the natural world and perfecting society. This term not only accurately describes the nature of the process but also points to its fundamental juxtaposition to secularization.

Of course, this single study has not been able to cover the wide range of subjects or the extensive historical materials affected by the needed reconceptualization. The primary intent has been to introduce the new concept and to use representative texts from the main lines of modern thought to demonstrate how the basic assumptions about modernity and secularization must be revised. Obviously, much more work remains to be done. At present, this work falls into three key areas. The first of these might be called problems in the history of modern historiography. The experience of the epochal break that creates modern consciousness also leads to a revision of the patterns of historical interpretation to bring them into conformity with this epochal experience. Despite the various theoretical and methodological advances in historical scholarship, these patterns have provided the basic categories of interpretation and established the basic points of transition and continuity within the modern period. As we have seen, developments in the history of science and other fields are beginning to break open the long-standing patterns and to introduce fundamental new questions and issues into the main lines of scholarship. The revaluations in Renaissance historiography now need to be extended to the assessment of the modern epoch as a whole. This reassessment can draw on the analyses by Löwith, Voegelin, and others, but the new studies must incorporate recent theoretical developments if they are to develop a perspective that can accommodate the growing body of historical data from the Renaissance and subsequent periods.

One work contributing to this new field is Paolo Rossi's *I segni del tempo*.[1] This study examines the reactions of seventeenth- and eighteenth-century historians and philosophers to geological and anthropological evidence of a time span considerably longer than the biblical tradition permitted. The data opened fresh approaches to historiography and the comparative analysis of ancient civilizations. Rossi shows that these materials also stimulated interest in Ancient Wisdom's myths and symbols of a Pre-Adamite time. According to the tradition, this Pre-Adamite time is followed by a period of alienation through the influence of the Judaeo-Christian tradition. This dark age is, in turn, superseded by a new age of enlightenment in which man regains his true humanity as a terrestrial god. This historical construction, obviously, reinforces Petrarch's conception of the medieval epoch as a "dark age" and the

1. Paolo Rossi, *The Dark Abyss of Time: The History of the Earth and the History of Nations from Hooke to Vico*, trans. Lydia G. Cochrane. Chicago, 1984.

Renaissance and Enlightenment celebration of a new age in which man (re)gains the knowledge and power to reign as a terrestrial god. Recognition of the renewed interest in the Pre-Adamite myths points to further flaws in the Löwith-Blumenberg debate over the legitimacy of modern interpretations of historical progress and suggests that a fundamental reconsideration of the eighteenth- and nineteenth-century historiography is needed.

The second field of study might be described as the interrelation of science and pseudo-science in the development of social science's epistemology and programs of reformation. This field would be the complement to work already done on the influence of experimental science on social science and the more recent revaluation of the influence of pseudo-science on modern science. Voegelin's studies have made an important contribution to this work; but, as we have seen, the analysis has to extend beyond Gnosticism to include the wide range of esoteric religious and pseudo-scientific traditions. As noted earlier, Voegelin's most recent writings moved in this direction, and there are also other scholars helping to open this field. Particularly notable are Klaus Vondung's *Magie und Manipulation* and David Walsh's *The Mysticism of Innerworldly Fulfillment*.[2]

A third area deserving attention is the relation of the Ancient Wisdom to the rise of utopian dreams of innerworldly fulfillment. While intellectual historians and political theorists have examined utopian writings as basic social and political speculation, they have not examined their foundations in the Ancient Wisdom and have not explored their connections with con- temporary political developments.[3] Frances Yates has opened this area of examination in *The Rosicrucian Enlightenment* and *Astraea*. Now, more detailed investigations, especially by political scientists, are needed in order to trace the influence of these utopias in the sixteenth and seventeenth centuries as well as in political thought and in political history. The

---

2. Klaus Vondung, *Magie und Manipulation: Ideologischer Kult und politische Religion des Nationalsozialismus* (Göttingen, 1971); and see David Walsh, *The Mysticism of Innerworldly Fulfillment: A Study of Jacob Boehme* (Gainesville, Fla., 1983).

3. For an overview, see the useful review essay by Lyman T. Sargent, "Is There Only Utopian Tradition?" *Journal of the History of Ideas*, XLIII (1982), 681–89; and Barbara Goodwin and Keith Taylor, *The Politics of Utopia: A Study in Theory and Practice* (London, 1982).

development of this field will make an important addition to conventional approaches that link modern political ideas to the work of Machiavelli and other sixteenth- and seventeenth-century secularists by providing further evidence that these ideas also derive from Agrippa, Bruno, Campanella, and others who were convinced that man could overcome his alienation and install a perfect social order.

The development of these areas will help open new historical perspectives on modernity that will in turn provide a more adequate understanding of its epochal consciousness and the characteristic features associated with it.[4]

4. My purpose here is to point to new directions to be taken, but it is also important to note briefly work in other areas complementary to this. The most important is the work on the continuation of the messianic, apocalyptic, and millenarian traditions in modern thought and experience. Major scholarly works in this field are listed in the Bibliography under "Utopian, Apocalyptic, and Millenarian Patterns." Recent studies that attempt to connect the utopian tradition with millenarianism are also listed.

Selected Bibliography

This study draws upon materials from several disciplines and historical periods. The bibliography groups the primary and secondary texts most pertinent to the major themes and issues treated in the text under three thematic headings: 1) Ancient Wisdom, 2) Renaissance, and 3) Modernity. The listings under each of these topics are grouped in the following order: a) primary texts and translations, b) commentaries and interpretive studies dealing specifically with the primary sources listed, and c) general studies or thematic interpretations pertinent to the subject as a whole. The only deviation from this format occurs in the subsection on Gnosticism and Modernity. Here, there is a further separation of sources so that primary texts and commentaries dealing specifically with ancient Gnosticism are listed first, followed by the sources dealing with modern Gnosticism.

It should be underscored that this is a bibliography of materials most directly related to the analysis in the text. A comprehensive listing on these major themes would be virtually impossible to prepare and almost impossible to use constructively. Students and scholars can use the following, how ever, as a guide to the subjects treated in the text and can draw upon these principal listings to follow the main lines of scholarship related to them.

Ancient Wisdom

HERMETIC MATERIALS: PRIMARY SOURCES

Corpus Hermeticum. 4 vols. Translated by A. D. Nock and A. J. Festugière. Paris, 1954–60. [Vols. I and II are the 2nd ed.]

Hermetica. 4 vols. Edited with English translation, introduction, and notes by Walter Scott. 1924–36; rpr. London, 1968.

COMMENTARIES AND INTERPRETIVE STUDIES

Festugière, A. J. *La Révélation d'Hermès Trismégiste.* 4 vols. Paris, 1949–54. [Vol. III is the 3rd ed.]

Luck, Georg, comp. and trans. *Arcana Mundi: Magic and the Occult in the Greek and Roman Worlds.* Baltimore, 1985.

Reitzenstein, Richard. *Poimandres: Studien zur griechisch-ägyptischen und frühchristlichen Literatur.* Leipzig, 1904.

Segal, Robert A. *The Poimandres as Myth: Scholarly Theory and Gnostic Meaning.* New York, 1986.

THEMATIC STUDIES

Benz, Ernst. *Les Sources mystiques de la philosophie romantique allemande.* Paris, 1968.

Blau, J. L. *The Christian Interpretation of the Cabala in the Renaissance.* Port Washington, N.Y., 1944.

Copenhaver, Brian P. *Symphorien Champier and the Reception of the Occultist Tradition in Renaissance France.* The Hague, 1978.

Evans, R. J. W. *Rudolf II and His World: A Study in Intellectual History, 1576–1612.* Oxford, 1973.

Fowden, Garth. *The Egyptian Hermes: A Historical Approach to the Late Pagan Mind.* New York, 1986.

Friedman, Jerome. *The Most Ancient Testimony: Sixteenth Century Christian-Hebraica in the Age of Renaissance Nostalgia.* Athens, Ohio, 1983.

Garin, Eugenio. *Astrology in the Renaissance: The Zodiac of Life.* Translated by Carolyn Jackson and June Allen. London, 1983.

Grese, William C. *Corpus Hermeticum XIII and Early Christian Literature.* Leiden, 1979.

Rossi, Paolo. *The Dark Abyss of Time: The History of the Earth and the History of Nations from Hooke to Vico.* Translated by Lydia G. Cochrane. Chicago, 1984.

Secret, François. *Les Kabbalistes chrétiens de la Renaissance.* Paris, 1964.

―――. *Le Zôhar chez les Kabbalistes chrétiens de la Renaissance.* Paris, 1958.

Shumaker, Wayne. *The Occult Sciences in the Renaissance: A Study in Intellectual Patterns*. Berkeley, 1972.

Tuveson, Ernest L. *The Avatars of Thrice Great Hermes: An Approach to Romanticism*. Lewisburg, 1982.

Viatte, Auguste. *Les Sources occultes du romantisme, illuminisme-théosophie, 1770–1820*. 2 vols. 1928; rpr. Paris, 1965.

Walker, D. P. *The Ancient Theology: Studies in Christian Platonism from the Fifteenth to the Eighteenth Century*. Ithaca, 1972.

Walsh, David. *The Mysticism of Innerworldly Fulfillment: A Study of Jacob Boehme*. Gainesville, Fla., 1983.

Renaissance

SECULARIZATION: PRIMARY TEXTS AND INTERPRETIVE SCHOLARSHIP

BOCCACCIO, Giovanni. *The Decameron*. Translated by G. H. McWilliam. Harmondsworth, Middlesex, 1972.

Serafini-Sauli, Judith. *Giovanni Boccaccio*. Boston, 1982.

GALILEI, Galileo. *Dialogo dei due massimi sistemi del mondo* [Dialogue concerning the two chief world systems]. 2nd ed. Translated by Stillman Drake. Berkeley, 1967.

———. "Letter to the Grand Duchess Christina." In *Discoveries and Opinions of Galileo*. Edited and translated with introduction by Stillman Drake. Garden City, N.Y., 1957.

MACHIAVELLI, Niccolò. *The Prince*. Edited and translated with introduction and annotation by James B. Atkinson. Indianapolis, 1976.

Baron, Hans. "Secularization of Wisdom and Political Humanism in the Renaissance." *Journal of the History of Ideas*, XXI (1960), 131–50.

Hexter, J. H. *The Vision of Politics on the Eve of the Reformation: More, Machiavelli, and Seyssel*. New York, 1973.

Mazzeo, J. A. *Renaissance and Revolution: The Remaking of European Thought*. New York, 1965.

———. *Renaissance and Seventeenth Century Studies*. New York, 1964.

Strauss, Leo. *Thoughts on Machiavelli*. Seattle, 1969.

SACRALIZATION: PRIMARY TEXTS AND INTERPRETIVE SCHOLARSHIP

AGRIPPA, Heinrich Cornelius. *De Incertitudine et Vanitate Scientiarum et Artium* [Of the vanitie and uncertaintie of artes and sciences]. Northridge, Calif., 1974.

———. *Opera*. Hildesheim, 1970.

Nauert, Charles G., Jr. *Agrippa and the Crisis of Renaissance Thought.* Urbana, Ill., 1965.

BRUNO, Giordano. *La Cena de le ceneri* [The Ash Wednesday supper]. Translated and edited by Edward A. Gosselin and Lawrence S. Lerner. Hamden, Conn., 1977.

———. *Dialoghi italiani.* 4th ed. Edited by G. Gentile. Firenze, 1957.

———. *Spaccio della bestia trionfante* [The expulsion of the triumphant beast]. Translated and edited by A. D. Imerti. New Brunswick, N.J., 1964.

CAMPANELLA, Tommaso. *La Città del Sole: Dialogo Poetico* [The city of the sun: A poetical dialogue]. Translated with introduction and notes by Daniel J. Donno. Berkeley, 1981.

FICINO, Marsilio. *Opera Omnia.* 4 vols. 2nd ed. 1576; rpr. Torino, 1959.

———. *De vita triplici* [The book of life]. Translated by Charles Boer. Irving, Tex., 1980.

———. *The Letters of Marsilio Ficino.* 3 vols. Translated by Members of the Language Department, School of Economic Sciences. London, 1978.

———. "Marsilio Ficino's Commentary on Plato's Symposium." Translated by Sears Reynolds Jayne. University of Missouri *Studies,* XIX (1944), 1–247.

———. *Théologie platonicienne de l'immortalité des âmes.* 3 vols. Translation and commentary by Raymond Marcel. Paris, 1964–70.

Allen, Michael J. B. *The Platonism of Marsilio Ficino: A Study of His "Phaedrus" Commentary, Its Sources and Genesis.* Berkeley, 1984.

———, ed. *Marsilio Ficino and the Phaedran Charioteer: Introduction, Texts, Translations.* Berkeley, 1981.

———, ed. and trans. *The Philebus Commentary.* Berkeley, 1975.

Cassirer, Ernst, P. O. Kristeller, and J. H. Randall, Jr., eds. *The Renaissance Philosophy of Man.* Chicago, 1948.

Collins, Ardis B. *The Secular is Sacred: Platonism and Thomism in Marsilio Ficino's "Platonic Theology."* The Hague, 1974.

Kaske, Carol V. "Marsilio Ficino and the Twelve Gods of the Zodiac." *Journal of the Warburg and Courtauld Institutes,* XLV (1982), 195–202.

Kristeller, P. O. *The Philosophy of Marsilio Ficino.* Translated by Virginia Conant. New York, 1943.

Moore, Thomas. *The Planets Within: Marsilio Ficino's Astrological Psychology.* Lewisburg, 1982.

Saitta, Giuseppe. *Marsilio Ficino e la Filosofia dell'umanesimo.* 3rd ed. Bologna, 1954.

Pico Della Mirandola, Giovanni. *De hominis dignitate, Heptaplus, De ente et uno.* Edited by Eugenio Garin. Firenze, 1942.

————. *Commentary on a Poem of Platonic Love.* Translated by Douglas Carmichael. Lanham, Md., 1986.

————. *Oration on Human Dignity.* Translated by Elizabeth Forbes in *The Renaissance Philosophy of Man,* edited by E. Cassirer, P. O. Kristeller, and J. H. Randall, Jr. Chicago, 1948.

Anagnine, Eugenio. G. *Pico della Mirandola: Sincretismo religioso-filosofico, 1463–94.* Bari, 1937.

Craven, William G. *Giovanni Pico della Mirandola: Symbol of His Age: Modern Interpretations of a Renaissance Philosopher.* Geneva, 1981.

Garin, Eugenio. *Giovanni Pico della Mirandola: Vita e dottrina.* Firenze, 1937.

Gautier-Vignal, L. *Pic de la Mirandole.* Paris, [1937].

Massetani, G. *La filosofia Cabbalistica di Giovanni Pico della Mirandola.* Empoli, 1897.

GENERAL SCHOLARSHIP

Baron, Hans. *The Crisis of the Early Italian Renaissance: Civic Humanism and Republican Liberty in an Age of Classicism and Tyranny.* Princeton, N.J., 1966.

Black, Robert. "Ancients and Moderns in the Renaissance: Rhetoric and History in Accolti's 'Dialogue on the Preeminence of Man in His Own Time.'" *Journal of the History of Ideas,* XLIII (1982), 3–32.

Butler, E. M. *The Fortunes of Faust.* Cambridge, England, 1952.

————. *Ritual Magic.* Cambridge, England, 1949.

Cassirer, Ernst. *The Individual and the Cosmos in Renaissance Philosophy.* New York, 1963.

Debus, Allen G. *The Chemical Philosophy: Paracelsian Science and Medicine in the Sixteenth and Seventeenth Centuries.* New York, 1977.

Eliav-Feldon, Miriam. *Realistic Utopias: The Ideal Imaginary Societies of the Renaissance, 1516–1630.* Oxford, 1982.

Ferguson, W. K. "The Interpretation of the Renaissance." In *Renaissance Essays: From the Journal of the History of Ideas,* edited by P. O. Kristeller and P. P. Wiener. New York, 1968.

French, Peter J. *John Dee: The World of an Elizabethan Magus.* London, 1972.

Garin, Eugenio. *La Cultura filosofica del rinascimento italiano: Ricerche e documenti.* Firenze, 1961.

————. *Italian Humanism: Philosophy and Civic Life in the Renaissance.* Translated by Peter Munz. New York, 1965.

———. *Medioevo e Rinascimento: Studi e ricerche*. Bari, 1954.

———. *Science and Civic Life in the Italian Renaissance*. Translated by Peter Munz. Garden City, N.Y., 1969.

———. *Testi umanistic su l'ermetismo*. Roma, 1955.

Gombrich, E. H. *Symbolic Images: Studies in the Art of the Renaissance*. 2nd ed. Oxford, 1978.

Jayne, Sears R. *John Colet and Marsilio Ficino*. [Oxford], 1963.

Kinsman, Robert S., ed. *The Darker Vision of the Renaissance: Beyond the Fields of Reason*. Berkeley, 1974.

Kristeller, Paul O. *Renaissance Concepts of Man: And Other Essays*. New York, 1972.

———. *Studies in Renaissance Thought and Letters*. Rome, 1956.

Levin, Harry. *The Myth of the Golden Age in the Renaissance*. Bloomington, 1969.

Merkel, Ingrid, and Debus, Allen G., eds. *Hermeticism and the Renaissance: Intellectual History and the Occult in Early Modern Europe*. Washington, D.C., 1987.

Molho, Anthony, and John Tedeschi, eds. *Renaissance Studies in Honor of Hans Baron*. DeKalb, Ill., 1971.

Mommsen, Theodor. *Medieval and Renaissance Studies*. Edited by Eugene Rice, Jr. Ithaca, 1959.

Panofsky, Erwin. *Meaning in the Visual Arts: Papers in and on Art History*. Garden City, N.Y., 1955.

———. *Renaissance and Renascences in Western Art*. Stockholm, 1960.

———. *Studies in Iconology: Humanistic Themes in the Art of the Renaissance*. 1939; rpr. New York, 1962.

Righini-Bonelli, M. L., and W. R. Shea, eds. *Reason, Experiment and Mysticism in the Scientific Revolution*. New York, 1975.

Robb, Nesca A. *Neoplatonism of the Italian Renaissance*. New York, 1968.

Thorndike, Lynn. *A History of Magic and Experimental Science*. 8 vols. New York, 1923–58.

Trinkaus, Charles. *In Our Image and Likeness: Humanity and Divinity in Italian Humanist Thought*. 2 vols. Chicago, 1970.

———. *The Poet as Philosopher: Petrarch and the Formation of Renaissance Consciousness*. New Haven, 1979.

———. *The Scope of Renaissance Humanism*. Ann Arbor, 1983.

Vickers, Brian, ed. *Occult and Scientific Mentalities in the Renaissance*. New York, 1984.

Walker, D. P. *Spiritual and Demonic Magic from Ficino to Campanella*. 1958; rpr. London, 1969.

Westman, Robert S., and J. E. McGuire, eds. *Hermeticism and the Scientific Revolution: Papers Read at a Clark Library Seminar, March 9, 1974*. Los Angeles, 1977.
Whittaker, Thomas. *The Neo-Platonists: A Study in the History of Hellenism*. 2nd ed. Cambridge, England, 1918.
Wind, Edgar. *Pagan Mysteries in the Renaissance: An Exploration of Philosophical and Mystical Sources of Iconography in Renaissance Art*. 2nd ed. New York, 1968.
Yates, Frances. *Astraea: The Imperial Theme in the Sixteenth Century*. London, 1975.
――――. *Giordano Bruno and the Hermetic Tradition*. London, 1964.
――――. "The Hermetic Tradition in Renaissance Science." In *Art, Science, and History in the Renaissance*, edited by C. S. Singleton. Baltimore, 1967.
――――. *Lull and Bruno*. London, 1982.
――――. *The Occult Philosophy in the Elizabethan Age*. London, 1979.
――――. *The Rosicrucian Enlightenment*. London, 1972.
――――. *The Valois Tapestries*. London, 1959.

Modernity

PRIMARY TEXTS AND COMMENTARIES
BACON, Francis. *Works*. 14 vols. Edited by James Spedding, R. L. Ellis, and D. D. Heath. London, 1857–74.
Lemmi, Charles. *The Classical Deities in Bacon: A Study in Mythological Symbolism*. New York, 1971.
Robertson, J. M., ed. *The Philosophical Works of Francis Bacon*. London, 1905.
Rossi, Paolo. *Francis Bacon: From Magic to Science* [Francesco Bacone: dalla magia alla scienza]. Translated by Sacha Rabinovitch. Chicago, 1968.
Weinberger, Jerry. *Science, Faith and Politics: Francis Bacon and the Utopian Roots of the Modern Age*. Ithaca, 1985.
Whitney, Charles. *Francis Bacon and Modernity*. New Haven, 1986.

COMTE, Auguste. *Cours de philosophie positive*. 6 vols. Paris, 1830–42.
――――. *The Positive Philosophy of Auguste Comte*. 2 vols. Translated by Harriet Martineau. London, 1853.
――――. *System of Positive Polity*. 4 vols. Translated by J. H. Bridges *et al.* London, 1875–77.
Gouhier, Henri. *La Jeunesse d'Auguste Comte et la formation du positivisme*. 3 vols. Paris, 1933–41.
Lévy-Bruhl, Lucien. *The Philosophy of Auguste Comte*. Translated by Kathleen de Beaumont-Klein. New York, 1903.

Mill, John Stuart. *Auguste Comte and Positivism*. London, 1908.

Standley, Arline Reilein. *Auguste Comte*. Boston, 1981.

MARX, Karl. *Karl Marx, Friedrich Engels: Historisch-kritische Gesamtausgabe, Werke, Schriften, Briefe*. 6 vols. Edited by D. Rjazanov [pseud.]. Frankfurt am Main, 1927–32.

———. *The Economic and Philosophic Manuscripts of Karl Marx*. Edited by Dirk J. Struik. Translated by Martin Milligan. New York, 1964.

———. *The German Ideology*. Edited by R. Pascal. 1947; rpr. New York, 1968.

Marx, Karl, and Friedrich Engels. *Basic Writings on Politics and Philosophy [by] Karl Marx and Friedrich Engels*. Edited by Lewis S. Feuer. Garden City, N.Y., 1959.

Kissin, S. F. *Farewell to Revolution: Marxist Philosophy and the Modern World*. New York, 1978.

Mazlish, Bruce. *The Meaning of Karl Marx*. New York, 1984.

Wessell, Leonard P., Jr. *Karl Marx, Romantic Irony, and the Proletariat: The Mythopoetic Origins of Marxism*. Baton Rouge, 1979.

———. *Prometheus Bound: The Mythic Structure of Karl Marx's Scientific Thinking*. Baton Rouge, 1984.

SECULARIZATION AND MODERNITY

Ausmus, Harry J. *The Polite Escape: On the Myth of Secularization*. Athens, Ohio, 1982.

Blumenberg, Hans. *The Legitimacy of the Modern Age*. Translated by Robert M. Wallace. Cambridge, Mass., 1983.

———. *Die Legitimität der Neuzeit*. 2nd ed. Frankfurt am Main, 1976.

———. "Progress, Secularization and Modernity: The Löwith/Blumenberg Debate." *New German Critique*, VIII–XIX (Winter, 1981), 63–79.

———. *Work on Myth*. Translated by Robert M. Wallace. Cambridge, Mass., 1985.

Charlton, Donald G. *Secular Religions in France, 1815–1870*. London, 1963.

Delekat, F. *Ueber den Begriff der Säkularisation*. Heidelberg, 1958.

Glover, Willis B. *Biblical Origins of Modern Secular Culture: An Essay in the Interpretation of Western History*. Macon, Ga., 1984.

Löwith, Karl. *From Hegel to Nietzsche: The Revolution in Nineteenth-Century Thought*. Translated by David E. Green. New York, 1964.

———. *Meaning in History: The Theological Implications of the Philosophy of History*. Chicago, 1949.

Lubac, Henri de. *The Drama of Atheist Humanism*. Translated by Edith M. Riley. Cleveland, 1963.

Lübbe, Hermann. *Säkularisierung: Geschichte eines ideenpolitischen Begriffs.* Freiburg, 1965.

Martin, David. *A General Theory of Secularization.* New York, 1978.

———. *The Religious and the Secular: Studies in Secularization.* New York, 1969.

Pagels, Elaine. *The Gnostic Gospels.* New York, 1979.

Stallman, M. *Was ist Säkularisierung?* Tübingen, 1960.

Taubes, Jacob, ed. *Gnosis und Politik.* München, 1984.

Zubel, Hermann. "Verweltlichung Säkularisierung: Zur Geschichte einer Interpretations-Kategorie." Dissertation, Munster, 1968.

ANCIENT GNOSTICISM AND MODERNITY

Hedrick, Charles W., and Robert Hodgson, Jr., eds. *Nag Hammadi, Gnosticism, and Early Christianity.* Peabody, Mass., 1986.

Jonas, Hans. *Gnosis und spätantiker Geist.* 2 vols. Göttingen, 1934–54.

———. *The Gnostic Religion: The Message of the Alien God and the Beginnings of Christianity.* 2nd ed. Boston, 1963.

Lacarrière, Jacques: *The Gnostics.* Translated by Nina Rootes. New York, 1977.

Martin, Luther H. *Hellenistic Religions: An Introduction.* New York, 1987.

Robinson, J. M., ed. *The Nag Hammadi Library in English.* New York, 1977.

Rudolph, Kurt. *Gnosis: The Nature and History of Gnosticism.* Translated and edited by Robert M. Wilson. San Francisco, 1983.

Scholer, David M. *Nag Hammadi Bibliography: 1948–1969.* Leiden, 1971.

Wilson, Robert M. *The Gnostic Problem.* New York, 1958.

Bloom, Harold. *The Flight to Lucifer: A Gnostic Fantasy.* New York, 1979.

Brooks, Cleanth. "Walker Percy and Modern Gnosticism." *Southern Review,* XIII (1977), 677–87.

Green, Henry A. *The Economic and Social Origins of Gnosticism.* Atlanta, 1985.

McKnight, Stephen A. "Understanding Modernity: A Reappraisal of the Gnostic Element." *Intercollegiate Review,* XIV (1979), 107–17.

Nador, György. *Spinoza, Kabbala, Gnosis: Schnneur Zalman in Zussamenhang.* London, 1976.

Sebba, Gregor. "History, Modernity and Gnosticism." In *The Philosophy of Order: Essays on History, Consciousness and Politics,* edited by Peter Opitz and Gregor Sebba. Stuttgart, 1981.

Voegelin, Eric. *From Enlightenment to Revolution.* Edited by John H. Hallowell. Durham, 1975.

———. *The New Science of Politics.* Chicago, 1952.

———. *Science, Politics and Gnosticism.* Chicago, 1964.

UTOPIAN, APOCALYPTIC, AND MILLENARIAN PATTERNS

Apocalyptic Spirituality: Treatises and Letters of Lactantius, Adso of Montier-en-Der, Joachim of Fiore, The Franciscan Spirituals, Savonarola. Translated by Bernard McGinn. New York, 1979.

Bauckham, Richard, ed. *Tudor Apocalypse: Sixteenth Century Apocalypticism, Millennarianism and the English Revolution.* . . . Oxford, 1978.

Billington, J. H. *Fire in the Minds of Men: Origins of the Revolutionary Faith.* New York, 1980.

Braunthal, Alfred. *Salvation and the Perfect Society: The Eternal Quest.* Amherst, 1979.

Cohn, Norman. *The Pursuit of the Millennium.* New York, 1957.

Davis, J. C. *Utopia and the Ideal Society: A Study of English Utopian Writing, 1516–1700.* Cambridge, England, 1980.

Dubos, Renée. *The Dreams of Reason: Science and Utopias.* New York, 1961.

Emmerson, Richard K. *Anti-Christ in the Middle Ages: A Study of Medieval Apocalypticism, Art, and Literature.* Seattle, 1981.

Garrett, Clarke. *Respectable Folly: Millenarians and the French Revolution in France and England.* Baltimore, 1975.

Gebhart, Jürgen. *Politik und Eschatologie: Studien zur Geschichte der hegelschen Schule in den Jahren 1830–1840.* München, 1963.

Gerber, Richard. *Utopian Fantasy: A Study of English Utopian Fiction Since the End of the Nineteenth Century.* London, 1955.

Goodwin, Barbara, and Keith Taylor. *The Politics of Utopia: A Study in Theory and Practice.* London, 1982.

Gottfried, Paul. *Conservative Millenarians: The Romantic Experience in Bavaria.* New York, 1979.

Hansot, Elisabeth. *Perfection and Progress: Two Modes of Utopian Thought.* Cambridge, Mass., 1974.

Lasky, Melvin J. *Utopia and Revolution: On the Origins of a Metaphor: or . . . Related.* Chicago, 1976.

Löwith, Karl. *Weltgeschichte und Heilsgeschehen: Die theologischen Voraussetzungen der Geschichtsphilosophie.* 2nd ed. Stuttgart, 1953.

Manuel, F. E., and F. P. Manuel. *Utopian Thought in the Western World.* Cambridge, Mass., 1979.

McGinn, Bernard. *Visions of the End: Apocalyptic Traditions in the Middle Ages.* New York, 1979.

More, Thomas. *Utopia: A New Translation, Backgrounds, Criticism.* Translated and edited by Robert Adams. New York, 1975.

Olson, Theodore. *Millennialism, Utopianism and Progress.* Toronto, 1982.

Reeves, Marjorie. *Joachim of Fiore and the Prophetic Future.* London, 1976.

Rhodes, James M. *The Hitler Movement: A Modern Millenarian Revolution.* Stanford, 1980.

Sargent, Lyman T. "Is There Only Utopian Tradition?" *Journal of the History of Ideas,* XLIII (1982), 681–89.

Schabert, Tilo. *Gewalt und Humanität: Ueber philosophische und politische Manifestationen von Modernität.* Freiburg, 1978.

Talmon, J. L. *The Myth of the Nation and the Vision of Revolution: The Origins of Ideological Polarisation in the Twentieth Century.* London, 1980.

———. *The Origins of Totalitarian Democracy.* London, 1952.

———. *Political Messianism: The Romantic Phase.* New York, 1960.

Tuveson, Ernest L. *Millennium and Utopia: A Study in the Background of the Idea of Progress.* Berkeley, 1949.

Vondung, Klaus. *Magie und Manipulation: Ideologischer Kult und politische Religion des Nationalsozialismus.* Göttingen, 1971.

West, Delno, and Sandra Zimdars Swartz. *Joachim of Fiore: A Study in Spiritual Perception and History.* Bloomington, 1983.

Yack, Bernard. *The Longing for Total Revolution: Philosophic Sources of Social Discontent from Rousseau to Marx and Nietzsche.* Princeton, 1986.

GENERAL STUDIES

Baumer, Franklin. *Modern European Thought: Continuity and Change in Ideas, 1600–1950.* New York, 1977.

Berman, Marshall. *All That Is Solid Melts into Air: The Experience of Modernity.* New York, 1982.

Bradbury, Malcolm, and James McFarlane, eds. *Modernism, 1890–1930.* Hassocks, Sussex, 1978.

Bury, J. B. *The Idea of Progress: An Inquiry into Its Origin and Growth.* New York, 1932.

Chefdor, M., R. Quinones, and A. Wachtel, eds. *Modernism: Challenges and Perspectives.* Urbana, 1986.

Dobbs, Betty J. *The Foundations of Newton's Alchemy: or, "The Hunting of the Greene Lyon."* Cambridge, Mass., 1975.

Galgan, Gerald. *The Logic of Modernity.* New York, 1982.

Jones, Richard F. *Ancients and Moderns: A Study of the Rise of the Scientific Movement in Seventeenth-Century England.* 2nd ed. St. Louis, 1961.

Kolb, David. *The Critique of Pure Modernity: Hegel, Heidegger and After.* Chicago, 1986.

McKnight, Stephen A. "The Renaissance Magus and the Modern Messiah." *Religious Studies Review,* V (1979), 81–89.

Passmore, J. *The Perfectibility of Man*. New York, 1970.

Redner, Harry. *In the Beginning Was the Deed: Reflections on the Passage of Faust*. Berkeley, 1982.

Weiss, Horace J., ed. *The Origins of Modern Consciousness: Essays by John Higham and Others*. Detroit, 1965.

Index

Adam's sin, as source of alienation in Agrippa and Bacon, 73, 75, 78, 94, 95

Adocentyn (Hermetic city), 44, 86, 99. See also *Picatrix*

Advancement of Learning, The (Bacon), 93–94 *passim*

Africa (Petrarch), 10–11

Agnoia, 24

Agrippa, Cornelius: Ancient Wisdom in works of, 71, 72, 74–79 *passim*; comments on Christianity by, 71, 73–74; Adam's sin and recovery in, 73, 75, 78; three paths to knowledge, 74–75; Cabalist tradition in works of, 74–77; criticisms of, 76–77; compared to Luther, Galileo, and Machiavelli, 78–79; mentioned, 7, 96, 104, 106. See also *De Incertitudine et Vanitate Scientiarum et Artium*; *De Occulta Philosophia*; *De Triplici Ratione cognoscendi Deum*

Alatiel. See Boccaccio, Giovanni: *The Decameron*

Alchemy, 96

Alcibiades (Plato), 68

Ancients and moderns, 91, 92, 101

Ancient theologians. See *Prisci theologi*

Ancient Wisdom: Recent scholarship on, ix–x; Renaissance understanding of, 20–22; Hermetism in, 41–45; in works of Ficino, 57; as synthesized by Pico, 67–70; criticisms of, by Agrippa, 76–77, 79; in works of Bruno, 79–82; in works of Bacon, 93; Pre-Adamite time, 110; relation to inner-worldly fulfillment, 111; mentioned, 3, 4, 15. See also Gnosticism, ancient; Hermetism; Sacralization

Anima mundi. See Ficino, Marsilio

Anthropos, 54. *See also* Magus; Terrestrial god

Apocalyptic tradition, 112*n*

Apollos: as disorder of philosophy in Bruno, 81, 82

Aristotelianism, 67

Asclepius: Hermetic view of God, man, and creation, 43, 44; in connection with Campanella, 86. *See also* "Egyptian Genesis"; Hermetism

Astrologers, and world spirit, 60

Astrology: compared with magic, 50, 57–64; mentioned, 85, 87. *See also* Campanella, Tommaso

Atlantis, myth of, 94

Augustine, Saint, 13

Bacon, Francis: Ancient Wisdom in works of, 93–96 *passim*; Cabalism in works of, 95; compared to Comte,